IMAGINATION

A psychological critique by

JEAN-PAUL SARTRE

TRANSLATED

WITH AN INTRODUCTION BY

FORREST WILLIAMS

Ann Arbor Paperbacks
THE UNIVERSITY OF MICHIGAN PRESS

First edition as an Ann Arbor Paperback 1972

ISBN 0-472-06185-2 (paperback)
ISBN 0-472-80666-1 (clothbound)
Published in the United States of America by
The University of Michigan Press and simultaneously
in Don Mills, Canada, by Longman Canada Limited
Manufactured in the United States of America

Introduction

The imagination has come in for more intensive study during the past three hundred years or so than ever before in the history of Western thought, and today problems concerning the nature of images are making themselves felt acutely in almost every area of inquiry, from anthropology to pedagogy, from mathematics to political theory. In at least one field, aesthetics, the imagination is frequently considered the central fact around which congregate the main difficulties and solutions. And yet the history of this intensive study of the imagination, Jean-Paul Sartre maintains, is the tale of a monumental error, appearing and reappearing in a dozen forms, sometimes gross, sometimes subtle. The error consists in a confusion, promoted by the assumption that images are things, between imagining and perceiving. A disastrous consequence for psychology of this confusion is to have rendered inexplicable the patently important role played by imagination in thinking.

The nature of the issue posed by Sartre may perhaps be illustrated rather broadly and briefly in our own language by the common term "after-image." Closing my eyes after looking out my window at the city of Rome, I am aware of what may be roughly described as a striped reddish patch, the so-called "after-image" of the sunlit scene. In the sense that a photographic film may be called an "image," the striped reddish patch is indeed a species of image. But what, then, are we to call the "image" of Pike's Peak which appears as I sit at my window in Rome? These two "images" are separated by all the difference between perception and imagination. For my so-called "after-image," the striped reddish patch, was no less an object of perception than the sunlit scene I saw before I closed my eyes. However, it was quite evident with regard to Pike's Peak that I was not perceiving it, but imagining it.

Our terms do not matter, of course, but the psychological distinctions our language expresses or fails to express do matter, at least within psychological theory. Whatever words one may care to use, my image from Rome of Pike's Peak is a type of mental phenomenon radically different from both my view of the scene before me and from any "after-image." The difference is not merely one of degree, or a matter of convention, as in our classifications of cumulus and cirrhus clouds, or flowers as contrasted with weeds. The difference is fundamental to the life of the human mind. However harmless the ambiguity of concepts betrayed by ordinary conversation, there ought to be no confusion on this point in any scientific theory of mental processes. For a psychology referring in any way to mental processes can never be worth more than its prior differentiation and characterizations of imagination, perception, reasoning, volition, aesthetic apprehension, and so forth. This truism has some far-reaching methodological implications, however.

As far as possible, an investigator must of course look at his subject matter in order to characterize it adequately. Thus, to appreciate and distinguish adequately the processes of mental life, of the "psyche," the psychologist must try to bring them into direct view. Consequently, he must undertake a reflexive inspection of consciousness, bending back awareness upon itself in order to discern characteristic structures and relationships of mental life. Around this requirement, there is no way. A purely external approach, the exclusive observation of behavior, becomes unthinkable. Thus, to return to the specific problem of Sartre's text, however much valuable information about the nature of the human imagination can be provided by observation of behavior, interviews, projective tests, and other important techniques of psychology, it is clear that at some juncture either observer or observed must introduce into the record some sort of first-hand account of imagination as it appears in reflection. The crucial question is whether this account will be rendered reluctantly and semiconsciously, subject to all the vagaries of ordinary language and everyday notions, or whether such a first-hand description will be made deliberately and methodically. If the mind fails to chart itself skillfully, a psychology of mental processes is impossible in anything but the most haphazard sense. This is as much as to say, in the terminology of Sartre and certain other contemporary philosophers, that a psychology of imagination must first of all be phenomenology. And Sartre therefore credits the first major contribution toward an adequate psychology of the human imagination to the late Edmund Husserl, twentieth-century pioneer of modern phenomenology and important figure in the formation of Gestalt psychology.

The position maintained by Sartre opposes those theories that somehow deduce the structure of mental functions from certain logical requirements of cognition, as was often tried in the seventeenth and eighteenth centuries. But the requirements of phenomenology are equally troubling to those contemporary thinkers who would simply equate science with the empirically confirmable, that is to say, with the sole evidence and authority of sense experience. The older view was right that not all truths are verifiable through the evidence of the senses, but wrong in supposing that deduction is the only alternative. The more current view is right in that one must indeed look to the evidence of experience, but wrong in supposing that all the experienceable data of science must be sense data. Only the recognition that there are structures of consciousness which can really be observed, but in reflection alone, rather than by the senses, permits a phenomenological approach to the nature of imagination.

In the absence of prior phenomenological elaboration, theories and investigations of the imagination could only proceed erratically, and were necessarily of short-term value. Yet to insist upon the rights and logical priority of phenomenology is not to claim that such analysis is exhaustive. Like any useful instrument, phenomenology cannot do all jobs. There are a multitude of problems concerning the nature of the imagination, Sartre very well knows, which can only be broached through investigations of a more usual kind, roughly comparable to the laboratory experiments of the physical sciences and yielding probable conclusions by a process of inductive generalization. The insistence is rather that before one can devise significant experiments regarding images, sense-perceptions, and so on, one must have as clear an idea as possible of what these matters are in the first place. Nor is it sufficient to reply that we all imagine absent friends, perceive the things before us, observe "after-images," and reason logically. If one considers Sartre's critique of many famous thinkers, it seems that there are egregious errors due to being too close to one's subject matter as well as to being too far from it. Consequently, the mere shift of attention from the objective side of experience to the subjective side, in the awkward and trusting manner of nineteenth-century introspectionism, must be rejected in favor of a highly methodical undertaking whose nature was first clearly grasped by Husserl in his revolutionary essay, *Ideas*. Psychology cannot, then, hope simply to muddle through, trying this or that experiment in a pluralistic spirit of cheerful indulgence toward anything dubbing itself a scientific investigation of the imagination. The unfortunate and characteristic result of such laxity of method is an unwitting introduction of some crude metaphysical dogma.

This last observation calls to mind that the dogmatic behaviorism of a generation ago no longer dictates to psychological theory, and a plea for a methodical phenomenology therefore need not fall on deaf ears in the psychological profession today. Nevertheless, the temper of contemporary psychology in the English-speaking world is hardly receptive to "philosophers'" claims. For one thing, having gained rather recently their administrative independence from academic departments of philosophy, the psychologists of our colleges and universities should feel a healthy aversion to anything hinting of a coalition with the professors of philosophy. Certainly nothing could be sounder than this desire for continued professional autonomy. One academic entanglement often seems burdensome to a seeker of truth, however much he may appreciate the social refuge provided by educational institutions; two would surely be depressing beyond all bounds. The issue posed by Sartre, however, has nothing at all to do with academic arrangements or the labels "psychologist" and "philosopher." What really matters regarding the important subject which Sartre treats in this book is that a true psychology of imagination be built on a foundation as substantial and nourishing as that of the natural sciences. Sartre claims that Husserl laid the cornerstone, and that further phenomenological inquiry is indispensable.

It might well be replied that the quickest way to establish such a promising foundation is widespread observation and experimentation of the sort already proven so successful in the natural sciences ever since men discarded preconceptions three centuries ago and began to observe the physical world. The surest path to loose and erroneous notions, it might be said, is precisely the avowedly "nonempiricist" approach proposed by phenomenological philosophy. This objection would appear to rest on the false assumption that the great advances in the natural sciences, for example, in physics, occurred when men at last opened their eyes and began seeing facts. This bizarre picture of scientific progress, promoted in many intellectual quarters nowadays, is likely to overlook not only the fact that a sufficient number of men have always been willing to heed experience, but the equally important fact that the imposing science of mathematics was first developed at length by geniuses and journeymen. Observation is indeed indispensable to any empirical science. But almost anyone, after all, can see and hear and reason. The crux of the revolution in physics was a more appropriate conceptual framework. The fruitful conceptions were provided by a science of essential relations and distinctions more fundamental than physics itself: a science of quantity, or, as was said in the seventeenth century, of extension. Owing to a current tendency virtually to identify mathematical thought with pure logic, the signal role of mathematics as a specific and nourishing foundation for empirical physics is easily overlooked. All the burden of empirical science is therefore placed upon some marvelous power of observation by which one simply "sees" and "hears" and "touches" facts (whatever that may mean). In reality, the assumption that empirical psychology will progress to the extent that it turns away from any prior inquiry not only has no support in the example of our most advanced science, but has been contradicted by physics over the past three centuries. To be sure, where a psychology of mental processes, for example, of imagination, is in question, this prior inquiry cannot be mathematics. The alternative is a phenomenological analysis, with no false pretension to that exactness which is desirable in some regions of fact but is inappropriate anyway to a psychology of imagination.

In a word: where one cannot import mathematical principles, one had better do one's prior categorizing of the field in a suitable fashion, with utmost deliberation and self-consciousness, for do it one will, either aptly or ineptly, either well or badly. Of such matters as imagination and perception, then, there can be no "plain empirical" psychology of the purely inductive sort often dreamed of yesterday and today, for something must do for such inquiries what mathematics does for physics. The program of a phenomenological psychology is precisely to establish, in the manner appropriate to the subject matter, an account of the major functions of consciousness in order to make possible meaningful accumulations of relevant experimental evidence. Sartre claims to show that theories of imagination from Descartes to the near present have been unable to perform this indispensable phenomenological task, short of which would-be experiments concerning the imagination remain in the dark about what on earth they propose to investigate. Even when a reflexive analysis has been attempted, the almost ineradicable prejudice which confounds imagination and perception has blinded thinker after thinker to the character of mental life. More often than not, no such attempt has really been made. As a result, Sartre claims, the most artificial "descriptions" by the most celebrated of thinkers—a Hume, a Bergson, a Taine, a Ribot, a Spaier, a Meyerson—have passed into book and journal as accredited psychological fact.

In the present work, Sartre assumed the role of critic of the history of psychology. On the foundations of this critique, Sartre went on to build both a psychology of the imagination and a more general theory of man which has become known as Sartrean Existentialism. The psychology of imagination, because it is a more limited topic, could withstand modifications of the more general theory of the human condition. Nevertheless, the two undertakings are related. Indeed, the present, critical work points toward the characterization of imagination, advanced in a subsequent book by Sartre, as a peculiarly negating activity. The more general implications for man and his world have in turn been presented in lengthier studies, as well as dramatized in fiction and plays.

If the French thinker is at all correct in his critical

assessment of the past three centuries of theories of the imagination, we have only just crossed the threshold of a significant conception of one of the most peculiarly human, and prized, of our endowments.

Forrest Williams
Istituto di Filosofia
University of Rome

Acknowledgments

The translator is most grateful for assistance given by Professors Paul Henle, Stanley Pullberg, and Pierre Delattre, as well as by the Council on Research and Creative Work of the University of Colorado.

Contents

I THE PROBLEM 1

II THE PRINCIPAL METAPHYSICAL SYSTEMS 7

III ASSOCIATIONISM 19

IV BERGSON 37

V BERGSONISM 59

VI THE WÜRZBURG SCHOOL 65

VII THE CLASSICAL POSTULATE 75

VIII THE CONTRADICTORY CONSEQUENCES OF THE CLASSICAL POSTULATE 85

A. *The Characteristics of "the True Image"* 85

B. *The Relations between Images and Thoughts* 104

C. *The Theory of Alain* 120

IX THE PHENOMENOLOGY OF HUSSERL 127

X CONCLUSION 145

NOTES 147

CHAPTER I

The Problem

I look at this white sheet of paper lying on my desk. I perceive its shape, its color, its position. These various qualities have traits in common. To begin with, they present themselves as beings whose existence in no way depends on my whim, as beings of which I can only take note. They exist *for* me, but they are not myself. Nor are they some other self. In other words, there is no spontaneity upon which they are dependent, neither mine nor that of any other consciousness.[1] They are at once present and inert. This inertness of the content of perception, which has often been remarked, is *being-in-itself*.

Nothing would be gained by debating whether this sheet of paper reduces to a collection of representations or whether it is and must be something more than that. What is certain is that I cannot spontaneously produce the white of which I take note. This inert shape, which stands short of all spontaneities of consciousness, which must be observed and learned about bit by bit, is what we call "a thing."[2] Never could my consciousness be a thing, because its way of being in itself is precisely to be *for* itself; for consciousness, to exist is to be conscious of its existence. It appears as a pure spontaneity, confronting a world of things which is sheer inertness. From the start, therefore, we may posit two types of existence. For it is indeed just insofar as things are inert that they escape the sway of consciousness; their inertness is their safeguard, the preserver of their autonomy.

But now I turn my head away. I no longer see the sheet of paper. I now see the gray wallpaper. The sheet of paper is no longer present, no longer *there*. I know perfectly well, however, that it has not annihilated itself: it is prevented by its inertness. It has just ceased to be *for me*.

Yet, here it is again. I have not turned my head. My gaze still falls upon the gray wallpaper. Nothing in the room has moved. Nevertheless, the sheet of paper appears to me once more, with its shape, its color, its location. And I know quite well, the instant it appears, that this is the very sheet of paper I was looking at a while ago. Is this truly that sheet of paper "in person"? Yes and no. To be sure, I readily acknowledge that it is the *same* sheet with the *same* qualities. But I know that that sheet of paper has remained over there: I know that I am not vouchsafed its presence. If I wish *really* to *see* it, I shall have to turn around toward my desk and redirect my gaze to the blotter where the paper is lying. The sheet appearing to me right now does share with the sheet I was looking at a while ago an identity in essence (by which I understand not only structure but individual character). But this essential sameness is not coupled with existential identity. Here is indeed the same sheet of paper—the one which at present is on my desk—but it exists differently. I do not *see* it. It does not assert itself as a limit to my spontaneity. Nor is it an inert datum existing *in itself.*[3] In a word, it does not exist *in fact,* it exists *as image*[4] [*en image*].

Unprejudiced self-examination would disclose that I distinguish quite spontaneously between what exists as thing and what exists as image.[5] I could not begin to enumerate these apparitions that we call "images," but, whether evoked voluntarily or not, they appear at once as something other than presences. I am never deceived on this matter. Indeed, anyone untutored in psychology would be quite surprised to be given a psychologist's explanation of images, and to be asked: Do you sometimes confuse the image of your brother with his actual presence? The recognition of an image as such is an immediate datum of inner sense, of inner experience [*du sens intime*].

It is one thing, however, to apprehend directly an image as image, and another thing to shape ideas regarding the nature of images in general. The only way to establish a true theory of the being of images is to propose nothing which does not have a direct source in reflective experience. For existence in the form of an image is in fact a mode of being most difficult to grasp. A mental struggle must be waged, particularly in order to rid oneself of the almost unshakeable habit of conceiving all modes of existence as physical in type. The confusion of modes of being is a special temptation in the present context. After all, the paper as image and the paper in reality are but one and the same sheet of paper on two different planes of being. Consequently, as soon as one shifts from pure contemplation of the image as such to thinking about images without forming them, one slides from essential identity of image and object to an alleged existential identity. Since the image, in this case, *is* the object, one draws the conclusion that the image exists in the same fashion as the object.[6]

Thus arises what we shall call "the naive metaphysics of the image." The image is made into a copy of the thing, existing as a thing. The sheet of paper "as image" is endowed with the same properties as the sheet of paper "in person": inert, it no longer exists solely for consciousness, but exists in itself, appearing and disappearing of its own accord rather than at the beck and call of consciousness. When no longer perceived, it does not cease to exist, leading instead a thinglike existence outside consciousness. This metaphysics—or rather, this naive ontology—is that of the man in the street. Hence the curious paradox: the very man who, without psychological sophistication, told us a while ago that he could directly recognize his images for images, now adds that he *sees* his images, that he *hears* them, etc. His first assertion derives from spontaneous experience, the second from a naively conceived theory. He fails to consider that were he to see his images, were he to perceive them as things, he could no longer distinguish them from objects; and so, in place of a same sheet of paper on two levels of being, he is left with two sheets of paper exactly alike and existing on the same plane. A perfect illustration of this naive, thing-ish view of images is provided by the Epicurean theory of simulacra. Things ceaselessly emit simulacra, "idols," which are simply coverings. These peelings have all the qualities of the object—content, shape, etc. Indeed, they just are objects. Once emitted, they exist in themselves, exactly like the emitting thing, and may travel about for an indefinite time.

Perception occurs when a sensory apparatus comes across one of these peelings and absorbs it.

Wholly a priori speculation having turned image into thing, inner intuition proceeds to tell us that the image is not the thing. The data of intuition are then incorporated in a new form into the theoretical construction. The image may be just as surely a thing as is the thing of which it is the image; but, by the very fact of being an image, it has a sort of metaphysical inferiority relative to the thing which it represents. In a word, the image is a lesser thing. The ontology of the image is now complete and systematic: the image is a lesser thing, possessed of its own existence, given to consciousness like any other thing, and maintaining external relations with the thing of which it is the image. It is obvious that nothing warrants the term "image" save this external relation and this vague and ill-defined inferiority (which could only be a magical sort of weakness, or on a different account a lesser degree of clarity and distinctness).[7] One may easily surmise all the contradictions that are bound to ensue.

Yet we shall unearth this naive ontology of images as a more or less implicit postulate of all the psychologists who have studied the subject. All, or almost all, have committed the confusion noted earlier between identity of essence and identity of existence. All have built a priori their theories of the image. And when finally they took to consulting experience, it was too late. Instead of allowing themselves to be guided by experience, they have forced experience to answer yes or no to leading questions. Doubtless a superficial perusal of the innumerable writings devoted in the past sixty years to the problem of the image seems to reveal an extraordinary diversity of viewpoints. We wish to show that beneath this diversity can be found a single theory. Deriving at first from the naive ontology noted above, it was brought to perfection by the great metaphysicians of the seventeenth and eighteenth centuries, under the influence of a variety of concerns foreign to the problem, and bequeathed to contemporary psychologists. Descartes, Leibniz, and Hume had one and the same conception of the image. They ceased to agree only when they went on to consider the relations of images to thoughts. Objectivistic psychology [*la psychologie positive* [8]] has kept the notion of the image just as it was left by these philosophers. And among the three solutions to the problem of the relation between images and thoughts proffered by these philosophers, no choice has been made, and none was possible. We propose to show that the case could not be otherwise the moment one accepts the postulate of a thing-image. To show this clearly, however, it is necessary to begin with Descartes and give a brief history of the problem of imagination.

CHAPTER II

The Principal Metaphysical Systems

The chief concern of Descartes, confronted by a Scholastic tradition that conceived species as semimaterial, semimental entities, was to draw a sharp line between mechanisms and thoughts, reducing the corporeal wholly to the mechanical. The image is a corporeal thing, the product of action on our body by external bodies by way of senses and nerves. Matter and consciousness being mutually exclusive, the image as physically imprinted somewhere on the brain could not be animated by awareness. It is an object, by the same title as external objects. To be exact, it is the limit of externality.

Imagination, or knowledge of the image, derives from the intellect, which, applied to the physical impression made in the brain, yields consciousness of the image. Moreover, the image does not stand before consciousness as a new object to be known, despite its physical status. The possibility of a relation between consciousness and its objects would thereby be postponed indefinitely. An image has the curious property of being able to motivate activities of the mind. Motions of the brain caused by external objects awaken in the mind ideas to which they bear no resemblance. These ideas do not come from the motions, for they are innate in man, appearing in consciousness when occasioned by motions. Such motions are as signs which provoke certain feelings in the mind. However, Descartes failed to develop this notion of a sign, by which he seemed to mean some arbitrary connection, and failed in particular to explain how there can be awareness of the sign. He seemed to allow for a transitive action between body and mind, which led to his introducing either a certain materiality into the mind or a certain mental character into the material image. Nor was it explained how the intellect applied itself to this special physical reality, the image; nor, for that matter, how imagination and body can intervene in thought—inasmuch as even bodies, according to Descartes, are apprehended by pure intellect.

The Cartesian theory does not enable us to distinguish sensations from memories or fancies, since there are the same cerebral motions in every case, whether the animal spirits are agitated by a stimulus from the external world,[1] from the body, or even from the mind. Only judgment and intellect permit us to decide, according to their intellectual coherence, which of our mirages correspond to existing objects.

Descartes thus limited himself to a description of what takes place in the body when the mind is thinking. He discussed the physical links connecting those physical realities called "images" and the mechanism which produces them. But Descartes had no notion of distinguishing thoughts in terms of these mechanisms which belong, like all other bodies, to the world of dubitable things.

Spinoza asserted even more pointedly than Descartes that the problem of true images cannot be resolved at the level of the image, but only by the intellect. As in Descartes his theory of images was severed from theory of knowledge and annexed to description of the body: an image is an affection of the human body. Chance, contiguity, and habit originate the links between images and memory, which is a physical revival of an affection of the body brought about by mechanical causes. The transcendentals and general ideas that constitute our vague experiences result from a confusion of images which itself is likewise physical in character. Imagination, or knowledge by images, differs profoundly from intellect, for it can forge false ideas, and presents truth only in a truncated form. Nevertheless, although contrasted to clear ideas, an image retains this much in common with them: it, too, is an idea. It is a confused idea, presenting itself as a degraded aspect of thought in which are expressed, nevertheless, the connections that obtain in the intellect. Imagination and intellect are not utterly distinct because passage from the one to the other is possible by an unfolding of the essences enfolded in images. Like knowledge of the first kind and knowledge of the third kind, like human bondage and human freedom, images and thoughts are at once cut off from each other and continuous with each other.

An image, for Spinoza, has two faces. As a thought of a man, who is a finite mode, it is fundamentally distinct from an idea, and yet, as a fragment of the infinite world which is the totality of ideas, it is an idea. Separated from thought, as in Descartes, the image tends also, as in Leibniz, to merge with thought, since the world of mechanical connections by which Spinoza described the world of the imagination is not cut off from the intelligible world.

The whole effort of Leibniz with respect to images was to establish continuity between these two modes of knowledge, image and thought. The image, for Leibniz, is suffused with the intellectual. Leibniz too described the world of imagination as sheer mechanism in which one cannot distinguish images as such from sensations, both of these expressing bodily states. To be sure, the associationism of Leibniz was no longer physiological, for images are preserved and interrelated in unconscious fashion in the soul. Only truths posited by reason sustain necessary relations, are clear and distinct. Thus there still survived here a distinction between the world of images, or confused ideas, and the world of reason. Their relation was conceived in the usual way. To begin with, the intellect is never pure because the body is always present to the soul. On the other hand, the image has only an accidental and subordinate role, the role of a sign, of a mere auxiliary to thought. Leibniz tried to develop this notion of a sign: it is an expression; that is to say, preserved within the image is the same system of relationships that obtains in the object of which it is the image, and transformation of either is expressible in a rule valid for the whole no less than for each part. Consequently, the sole difference between image and idea is that in the one case the expression of the object is confused, in the other case, clear. Confusion results from the fact that every motion enfolds within itself the infinitude of motions of the universe. The brain receives an infinity of modifications, to which can correspond only confused thought, embracing the infinity of clear ideas that would correspond to each detail. The clear ideas are thus contained in the confused idea, unconscious, perceived without being apperceived. Only the sum total is apperceived, and is simple in appearance owing to our ignorance of its components. The difference between image and idea, therefore, is very nearly reducible to a purely mathematical one: the image has the opaqueness of the infinite, the idea has the clarity of a finite and analyzable quantity. Both are expressive.

But if the image reduces to unconscious elements in themselves rational, to an infinity of expressive relations, thereby sharing in the dignity of thought, its subjective aspect becomes inexplicable. How does the sum of unconscious perceptions of, for example, yellow and blue, yield the conscious apperception of green? How by a diminution in our awareness of these elementary ideas can their co-presence in the mind produce these sudden combinations? Untroubled by this difficulty, Leibniz tried to find a meaning in the image which would annex it to thought and dispel the image as such. Moreover, he misused a mathematical analogy by taking for granted that confusion equals infinity equals opacity or even irrationality. The irrational of a mathematician is indeed nothing but some rational which we do not yet know how to assimilate; but a logical construction could never end in an absolutely alogical opaqueness on which thought has no purchase. Quality is not quantity, not even infinite quantity. Leibniz never managed to reinstate the sensory character of sensation, its qualitativeness, of which he had earlier robbed it. Moreover, the notion of expression, which allowed him to attribute an intellectual significance to sensory data, is obscure. Expression is an ordered relation, asserted Leibniz, a correspondence. But there can be no natural representation by one "realm" of another "realm."[2] There would always have to be an arbitrary mental interpretation in order for the mind to acknowledge subsequently that it is confronted by equivalent relationships.

In attempting, therefore, to establish the representational value of the image, Leibniz failed to describe clearly the relation of image to object and failed to account for the original character of its existence as an immediate datum of consciousness.

Whereas Leibniz tended to discount the image as such in order to resolve the Cartesian opposition between image and thought, the empiricism of Hume strove rather to put all thought to the account of a system of images. Hume borrowed from Cartesianism its description of the mechanistic world of the imagination, and isolated this world both from the physiological base in which it was rooted and from the intellect above, thus making it the sole level on which the human mind really functions. In the mind there exist only impressions and copies of these impressions. The latter are ideas, preserved in the mind by a sort of inertia. Ideas and impressions do not differ in kind, hence a perception is not as such distinguishable from an image.[3] To tell them apart one would have to resort to an objective criterion of coherence, of continuity. The meaning of the criterion is far more obscure than in Descartes, for in a mind consisting solely of a mosaic of impressions, the leverage for emerging from impressions and for rising above them becomes inconceivable.

Images are linked by relations of contiguity and resemblance that act like "given forces," clustering by attractions of a semimechanical, semimagical nature.

The similarity of certain images allows us to assign them a common name which leads us to believe in the existence of the corresponding general idea. Only the set of images is real, however, having "potential" existence in words.[4]

This entire theory presupposed a notion which was never mentioned, the notion of an unconscious. Ideas exist only as internal objects of thought, yet they are not always conscious, awakening only because of a connection with conscious ideas. They stay in existence, therefore, in the manner of physical objects. Although always there in the mind, not all ideas are perceived. Why? And how is it that being pulled by a given force toward a conscious idea makes an idea conscious? Hume never posed this problem. The being of consciousness simply vanished behind a world of opaque objects endowed—we know not from whence—with a sort of phosphorescence, capriciously distributed and performing no active function. Moreover, to reconstruct the whole of thought by means of images, associationism was obliged to acknowledge the existence of an entire class of thoughts whose objects, as the Cartesians had quite well realized, are not given by any sensory impression at all.

By the end of the first half of the eighteenth century, therefore, the problem of the image had been succinctly formulated, and three solutions had crystallized.

Shall we say, with the Cartesians, that there exists pure thinking always capable—by right, at least—of taking the place of the image, as truth replaces error, as the adequate replaces the inadequate? In this case, we do not have an image world and a world of thought, but an incomplete, truncated, purely pragmatic mode of apprehension of the world, and another mode of apprehension, a total and disinterested vision. The image is the realm of appearance, but appearance which our human condition invests with a sort of substantiality. Thus there exists a veritable hiatus, at least at the psychological level, between image and idea. Image proves to be indistinguishable from sensation, or rather, the distinction to be established between image and sensation will be primarily of practical value. A shift from the imaginative level to the ideational is always a leap. Here is a fundamental discontinuity which necessarily implies a philosophical revolution—or, as it is still the custom to say, a philosophical "conversion"—so radical as to raise the question of the very identity of the subject. Viewed psychologically, a special synthetic form is needed to unite *in one and the same consciousness* the self that thinks the wax and the self that imagines it, and concurrently to unite the conceived wax and the imagined wax in the assertion of identity, "It is the *same* object."[5] On essential grounds, the image could provide thought with only the most suspect sort of assistance. Problems there are which present themselves only to pure thought, because their terms could in no way be imagined. Other problems allow the use of images provided their employment be strictly regulated. In any event, such images have no other function than to ready the mind to perform the conversion. Used as schemata, as signs, as symbols, they never enter as real elements into the act of ideation properly so-called. Left to themselves, they succeed each other according to a purely mechanical type of connection. Psychology finds itself relegated to the region of sensations and images. Assertion of the existence of pure thought removes the intellect even from psychological description; the intellect can only be a subject of epistemological and logical investigation of meanings.

But the independent existence of meanings might be regarded as nonsense. For they would have to be supposed to exist a priori in thought, or else interpreted as Platonic entities. In both cases they would elude inductive science. Should one wish to assert the rights of an objective science of human nature ascending from facts to laws, as in physics or biology, should one wish to treat psychic facts [6] as *things,* then one ought to renounce this world of essences given to intuitive contemplation, this world of essences in which generality is given from the start. A methodological axiom becomes necessary: we can arrive at no law without first passing through facts. But by a legitimate application of this axiom to theory of knowledge, one would be bound to acknowledge that the laws of thought, too, issue from facts, that is to say, from psychological sequences. Logic thus becomes a part of psychology.[7] The Cartesian image becomes, for inductive purposes, the individual fact. The epistemological principle, "Begin with the facts in order to derive the laws" becomes the metaphysical principle, *Nihil est in intellectu quod non fuerit prius in sensu.*[8] Thus does the Cartesian image appear simultaneously as the individual object with which the scientist must begin, and as the primary element which through combination produces thought, that is to say, the host of logical meanings. One is brought to the panpsychologism of Hume. Psychic facts are individualized things connected by external relations, and thought must have a *genesis.* Thus, the Cartesian superstructures collapsed, and only the thing-image remained.

But with the collapse of these superstructures crumbled also the synthesizing power of the self and the very notion of representation. Associationism was first and foremost an ontological doctrine asserting the radical identity of the mode of being of psychic facts and the mode of being of things. In fine, only things exist. They enter into relations with each other and thereby constitute a certain grouping which we call *consciousness*. The image is nothing but the thing in a certain type of relation with other things. We may discern here the seed of American Neo-Realism. Yet all these assertions, methodological, ontological, and psychological, flow analytically from the abandoning of Cartesian essences. While the intelligible heaven was falling, the image did not become something other than it had been, underwent no modification at all, for the good reason that for Descartes the image was already a thing. Such was the advent of psychologism, which in its various guises is nothing but an objectivistic [9] anthropology, that is to say, a science that would treat man as a being of the world by ignoring the essential fact: that man is also a being who represents the world to himself and represents himself in the world.[10] This objectivistic anthropology was already sown in the Cartesian theory of images. Adding nothing to Cartesianism, it only subtracted. Descartes posited at once images and imageless thoughts; Hume kept the images without the thoughts.

But one might wish to keep everything embraced in a psychical continuity, asserting the homogeneity of fact and law and demonstrating that pure experience is already reason. In that case, one would point out that if we can pass from fact to law, it is because the fact was already, as it were, an expression of the law, a sign of the law—or rather, the fact is the law itself. Nothing would remain of the Cartesian distinction between necessary essence and empirical fact. Rather, one would rediscover the necessary in the empirical. No doubt the fact *appears* to be contingent. Doubtless no human intelligence could give a rational accounting of the color or shape of this sheet of paper.[11] But this is so only because human intelligence is by nature limited. Induction takes place only where *by right* we should deduce. The "contingent truths" of Leibniz are *in principle* necessary truths. Thus the image remains for Leibniz a fact like other facts. The chair in image is the chair in reality, nothing else. But just as the chair in reality is a confused cognition of a truth reducible *in principle* or *de jure* to an identity-proposition, so the image is only a confused thought. In a word, the solution of Leibniz is indeed a pan-logicism, save that this pan-logicism has only an existence *de jure,* superimposed upon the empirically actual. Psychologically speaking, one would have to seek out beyond every image the thought which in principle it implies, but never would the thought itself be revealed to an actual intuition [*à une intuition de fait*].[12] Never could one have concrete experience of the pure thought as in the Cartesian system. This is why Leibniz could reply to Locke with the famous phrase: *nisi ipse intellectus.*[13] When all is said and done, the image of the empiricists reappeared here as such, as a psychological fact, and the disagreement between Leibniz and Locke concerned only its metaphysical status.

Such were the three solutions offered by the three great currents of classical[14] philosophy: a reign of thought radically different from that of images; a world of pure images; and a world of fact-images, behind which must lie thought, appearing only indirectly as the sole possible reason for the organization and the teleology discernible in the world of images (somewhat as God can be concluded in the physicotheological argument from the order of the world).

Throughout these three solutions, the image retained the same structure: it remained *a thing*. Only its relations to thought were modified, according to the point of view taken on the relations of man to the world, of the universal to the particular, of existence as object to existence as representation, of mind to body. It may be that we shall find, as we trace the continuous development of the theory of images through the nineteenth century, that these three solutions are the only possible answers the moment one accepts the postulate that an image is but a thing—that they are equally possible solutions and equally defective solutions.

CHAPTER III

Associationism

Romanticism might have spelled the complete regeneration of the problem of images, for in philosophy, as in politics and literature, it manifested itself by a return to the synthetic sensibility, to the notions of faculties, order and hierarchy, to mental realities coupled with a vitalistic psychology. Indeed, for some time the manner of envisaging the image did seem quite different from the three classical viewpoints we have enumerated. Many first-rate minds, wrote Binet,

> resisted any admission that thought needs material signs in order to function. This seemed to them a concession to materialism. In 1865, during the time in which much debate on hallucinations was taking place in medical-psychological circles, the philosopher Garnier and eminent alienists such as Baillarger, Sandras and others still maintained that an unbridgeable chasm separates the conception of an absent or imaginary object—in other words, an image—and a real sensation produced by an object which is present. These two phenomena were said to differ not only in degree, but in their very nature.[1]

Doubt was thus being cast on the postulate shared by the positions of Descartes, Hume, and Leibniz: the identical nature of image and sensation.[2] Unfortunately, rather than the termination of a doctrine, it was a matter of general atmosphere, as we know; and the atmosphere soon changed. Even in 1865, the thinkers cited by Binet could already be viewed as conservative. "The idea of science," wrote Giard, "is intimately linked to the ideas of determinism and mechanism." A mistake, no doubt; but this deterministic and mechanistic science was what conquered the generation of 1850.

Moreover, mechanism means the analytical spirit. Mechanism attempts to resolve a system into its elements and implicitly accepts the postulate that these remain strictly the same whether in isolation or in combination. Naturally, a further principle follows: the relations entertained by the elements of a system are external—a postulate ordinarily formulated under the title of the principle of inertia. For the intellectuals of the period which we are considering, to adopt a scientific attitude toward something—whether a physical body, an organism, or a fact of consciousness—was to suppose, prior to all investigation, that the object in question is a combination of inert invariants in external relations. By an odd detour, whereas the science of scientists, science "on the march," is in essence neither pure analysis nor pure synthesis, adapting its methods to the nature of the object,[3] an oversimplified interpretation of scientific advances brought philosophers back to the Critical[4] viewpoint of the eighteenth century, and revived as a matter of principle hostility to the spirit of synthesis. Henceforth, every attempt to establish a scientific psychology was necessarily tantamount to an attempt to reduce psychic complexity to some mechanism.

> **The words "faculty," "power," "capacity," which have played so large a role in psychology are, we shall see, but convenient terms for gathering all the facts of a distinct kind into a distinct species. . . . They designate no mysterious, profound essence which subsists and hides beneath the flux of facts. . . . Thereby psychology becomes a science, for our cognitions are facts. We can speak with precision and in detail of a memory, an anticipation, just as of a vibration, a physical movement. . . . The subject of science everywhere today consists of minute, well-chosen facts, important and meaningful, well-attested in all their circumstances and minutely inspected. . . . Our major concern is to know what are the elements, how they are generated, in what ways and under what conditions they combine, and what are the constant effects of such combinations. Such is the method we have attempted to pursue in this work. In the first part, we have separated out the elements of cognition; by reduction after reduction we arrived at the simplest elements; then, we passed to the physiological changes which are the condition of their origin. In the second part, we have first described the mechanism and general effect of their combination. Then, applying the law we discovered, we have examined the elements, the formation, the certitude, and the scope of the main types of knowledge.[5]**

Thus did Taine envisage the constitution of a scientific psychology in the Preface to his book, *De l'Intelligence* [*On Intelligence*], published in 1871. One notes a clear-cut abandonment of the principles of psychological investigation set forth by Maine de Biran. The ideal was now to be able to view a psychic fact as "a physical motion." Consequently, we see coexisting in the same text the purely methodological and unimpeachable principle of consulting experience[6] ("minute, well-chosen facts," etc.) and a metaphysical theory, introduced a priori, concerning the nature and goals of experience. Taine did not limit himself to recommending liberal use of experience. He decided on the basis of unchecked principles *what the experience must be,* describing the results before consulting experience. Naturally, the description involved a host of hidden assertions concerning the nature of the world and existence in general. One may wonder, after reading these opening pages, whether the innumerable facts about to be presented—almost all of them false, by the way—will do more than mask a purely logical chain of concepts.

A reading of the book unfortunately confirms these misgivings. Nowhere, it is fair to say, does one find a concrete description, a comment dictated by observation of facts. At every turn is a construct. Taine used first a reductive analysis, and thanks to this method leaped naively and unsuspectingly from the psychological level to the physiological level, the latter being simply the territory of sheer mechanism. Next, he turned to synthesis. But in this case "synthesis" meant mere recombination. One goes back from relatively simple groupings to more complex ones. The trick has been turned: the physiological is ushered into consciousness.

> **There is nothing real in the self save the series of occurrences. Of varying aspect, these are in their nature all alike, and can all be reduced to sensation,**

> which, considered from the outside by the indirect method known as "external perception," reduces to a set of molecular motions.[7]

And the image, the essential element of psychic life,[8] will appear at its appointed hour in this reconstruction to occupy a niche carved out in advance.

> Everything in the mind that exceeds "raw sensation" is reducible to images, that is to say, to spontaneous repetitions of sensation.

Thus was the very nature of the image deduced a priori. Not for one second were the data of inner experience consulted. From the start we are supposed to know that an image is merely a resuscitated sensation, that is, in the end, "a set of molecular motions." This was to posit the image as an inert invariant, and by the same token to liquidate the imagination. The mind is a "polypary of images": such is the final word of analytical psychology. But Taine failed to realize that such was also his initial postulate. The two massive volumes of *De l'Intelligence* merely develop in fastidious fashion the simple statement cited earlier: "Our major concern is to know what are the elements, how they are generated, in what ways and under what conditions they combine . . ."[9]

This principle once assumed, it remained only to explain how images combine to give birth to concepts, to judgment and to reasoning. Taine naturally borrowed his explanations from associationism. Hume, more skillful, at least had attempted to conjure up a ghost of experience. Hume did not wish to *deduce*. Furthermore, Hume's laws of association stand, or at least seem to stand, on the terrain of pure psychology, as links between phenomena such as they *appear* to the mind. Taine was led by an initial confusion between experience and analysis to set up a hybrid associationism, now formulated in physiological terms, now in psychological language, now in both at once. Thus, his purely theoretical empiricism was coupled with a metaphysical realism. Hence a paradoxical contradiction: in order to erect a psychology after the model of physics, Taine adopted the associationist conception which, as Kant had shown, ends in a radical denial of science as legislative; yet, while he was unwittingly destroying on the psychological level the very notion of necessity and the very concept of science, he clung on the level of physiology and physics to a system of necessary laws. Since he maintained that the physiological and the psychic are but two sides of the same reality, it followed that the connections of images as facts of consciousness—the only connections which appear to us—are contingent, whereas the connecting of molecular motions which makes physical realities of them is necessary. Thus, what was assumed for a long time to be empiricism was only a metaphysical realism misfired.

But the ideas of Taine, seductive in their scientific apparel, were receiving confirmation on all sides. The investigations of Galton [10] were bringing new factual demonstrations. At the same time, from 1869 to 1885, Bastian, Broca, Küssmaul, Exner, Wernicke, and Charcot laid down the classical theory of aphasia, which inclines to nothing short of differentiated centers of imagery. Even in 1914, Dejerine was supporting this view. Other psychologists—such as Binet in his first period [11]—attempted to conquer new territories for associationism. The physicalist metaphor which makes the image into "the survival of a disturbance beyond the stimulus which generated it," and which assimilates images to pendulum oscillations occurring long after displacement from the point of equilibrium by an outside force—this metaphor and many others of the same sort had remarkably successful careers. Following John Stuart Mill, Taine and Galton had definitively established the nature of the image: it is a reviving sensation, a solid fragment snapped off from the external world. Whatever the subsequent viewpoint of any psychologist, the notion of the image as a resuscitation was always to be implicitly assumed. And the very psychologists who were to insist on the existence of psychic syntheses were nonetheless to hold fast, under the heading of supportive elements or survivals, to the atoms bequeathed them by analytical psychology.

Indeed, about 1880, a new generation of philosophers was to define its position *in the light of* and *over against* associationism. The ideas of Taine and Mill were not rejected for the sake of a return to inner experience. Rather, influenced by a variety of factors, they wished both to preserve these ideas and to transcend them in a larger synthesis.

Among the chief reasons for this change must be cited the growing success of Kantian thought, of which Lachelier made himself the champion in France.[12] From this viewpoint, the philosophers could put themselves the following sort of question: how reconcile, on the plane of psychology, the data of experience and the exigencies of a critique of knowledge? But the significant thing was that Taine's descriptions were regarded as drawn from experience. It was only a question of interpreting them. No one doubted that there were atom-images. This was a *fact.* Indeed, that experience reveals nothing but such images, many philosophers were happy to acknowledge. But, apart from the question of fact, there was a question of right, of principle. By right, there had to be something else: a thought which at every moment organizes and transcends the image. The problem, then, was to rediscover, behind what is there in fact, what must in principle be there.

Reasons of a wholly different sort, moreover, were working in support of this point of view. Political and social ideas had changed. A critical individualism was now distrusted because of its moral consequences. It led to anarchy in politics, and to materialism and atheism. For there occurred in France at this time a strong conservative reaction. The notions of order and social hierarchy returned in full force. At the Versailles Assembly, censure was meted out to "radical thinkers . . . [who] do not believe in God, and in [whose] writings one finds definitions of man that degrade our species." [13] The Assembly roundly denounced the "detestable doctrines" of the radicals. Frightened by the Commune, the conservative bourgeoisie turned again to Religion, as in the first part of the reign of Louis-Philippe. Hence the necessity for the incumbent intellectuals to combat in every quarter the analytical tendency of the eighteenth century. Above the individual must be posited synthetic realities, the family, the nation, the society. Above the individual image must be reasserted the existence of concepts, of thought. Hence the subject for the competition proposed on April 30, 1882, by the *Académie des Sciences Morales et Politiques:*

> To expound and discuss the philosophical doctrines that reduce the faculties of the human mind, and even the self, to the fact of association alone. To reinstate the laws, the principles and the realities which the doctrines in question tend to suppress.

Thus, official science gave the starting signal. But even from this standpoint there was no notion of denying the existence of sensory images and laws of association. Ferri, prize winner in the competition, wrote:

> Pure thought is no illusion, for it apprehends itself in the reflective consciousness of concepts and intellectual processes, *though by an effort of meditation and abstraction.* In reality, the brain never ceases to work on behalf of pure thought, furnishing it with visible, audible and tangible phantoms, materials on which pure thought impresses its form.

The passage is striking. None could better show the uncertainties of introspective knowledge.[14] An author dedicated to refuting associationism was so imbued with the theories he wanted to combat that he gave them the blessing of experience and was able to discover in himself only particular images. That activity of thought appeared to him only after *an effort of abstraction.* He asserted thought in some sense *over against* experience. Thirty years later, as we shall see, everyone will readily find, or will think he has found, imageless states in the most paltry intellectual process.

No doubt this timidity arose in part from the enormous success of the writings of Taine. But there was more to it than that. The reaction to associationism was led chiefly by conservative Catholicism, for which a theory of the image has a religious aspect not to be ignored.

Man is a compound, as Aristotle had said, of thought closely united to body. There is no thought unblemished by the corporeal. The Cartesian notion of pure thought, that is to say, an activity of the soul that could function without the aid of the body, is heretical pride. This is the reason Jacques Maritain could align Descartes with Protestantism. Thus, we are brought back to Aristotle, with his claim that no intellectual activity could be undertaken without the help of the imagination; [15] and to Leibniz who, Protestant though he was, was always far closer to Catholic thought than was Descartes. We see why associationism was not rejected: it merely needed to be reintegrated. Associationism means the body, the weakness of man. Thought is his dignity. But dignity is never without weakness; thought is never without images. This was the spirit in which R. P. Peillaube wrote in 1910 in his book, *Images:*

> Images are necessary to the formation of concepts. There is not one concept that is innate. Abstraction has precisely the goal, in its original and generative function with respect to the intelligible, of raising us above the image and enabling us to think its object in a universal and necessary form. Our mind cannot directly conceive anything intelligible except the abstractly intelligible, which can only be produced from the image and with the image by intellectual activity. All the material capable of being exploited by the intellect is of sensory and imaginative origin. . . .

Of a sudden, the Leibnizian doctrine on the relation of image to thought has reappeared. True, in this case the doctrine did not have all the profundity to be found in Leibniz, but writers specifically appealed to it. Indeed, this was the doctrine determining the particular nuance of philosophy at the close of the century. It was surely Leibniz from whom the notion was derived that at all times thought is present yet inaccessible to inner experience. We have already met this notion in Ferri, and Brochard was to be even more specific:

> ***Because*** **the object is alterable,** ***I know*** **that the image is not equivalent to my concept. What the concept contains in addition is, in the words of Hamilton, a character of potential universality. Thought, constrained to assume a sensory form, appears momentarily as being such and such an object, such and such a particular example, resting in it, as it were; yet thought is not imprisoned there or absorbed. Transcending the images which express it, thought is able to incarnate itself later in other, more or less different images.[16]**

We arrive in this way at a peculiar conception of thinking. Since the datum of introspection is an image, thought has no real, concrete existence accessible to immediate awareness. It has no universality *in actus,* otherwise it could be apprehended directly; rather, it has a *potential* universality which one may *infer* from the fact that a word can be accompanied by quite different images. Extending through these particular images is a sort of rule that governs their selection. But there is no "consciousness of a rule" in the sense later encountered in the Würzburg School.[17] The rule—which is the concept—is given only in a particular image as the mere possibility of replacing this image by another, equivalent image.

Thus, for Brochard consciousness wears the same dress as in Taine: there are images, and there are words.

But in place of the bond of sheer habit Taine posited between images, Brochard and many of his contemporaries introduced a functional connection, to wit: thought. And yet, even if this substitution enabled them to reinstate all of rationalism, it was no less true that this bizarre thought floated, murky to itself, between existence in principle and existence in fact. Better said: Thought exists as function, but not as awareness. Revealed only by its effects, thought was not even defined by the transition from a present image to another image, but by the mere *possibility* of effecting such a transition. And if this possibility is not actually present to consciousness, this is because it is a purely logical possibility, at most revealing itself to reflection in the form of an insufficiency of the image as such.

Such was the timid attempt of the rationalist revival to combat associationism. It saw itself pinned between the alleged data of introspection ("In consciousness there are only images and words") and the alleged findings of physiology (cerebral localizations). Therefore, it surrendered to Taine the province of facts and took refuge on the level of Criticism. In such wise had Leibniz once replied to Locke: *Nihil est in intellectu quod non prius in sensu nisi ipse intellectus.* In such wise had Kant replied to Hume: "It may well be that on the ground of experience one can find no link between the cause and the effect save empirical succession. But for experience to be possible, synthetic a priori principles must constitute it."

This reply, allowable in connection with the constituting of experience, is inadmissible when it is a matter of taking account of thought within experience. The thinking at issue is not constitutive thought, but a concrete activity of man, a phenomenon constituted in the midst of other phenomena. It is one thing to constitute my present perception (a room, books, etc.) by categorial syntheses through which consciousness *is rendered possible.* It is another thing to frame conscious thoughts upon this perception *once constituted* (for example, to think: The books are on the table, This is a door, etc.). In the second case, consciousness exists confronting the world. Therefore, if I frame a thought about the world, the thought must appear to me as a real psychic phenomenon. There is no question here of "virtuality," nor of "possibility." Consciousness is act, and everything that exists in consciousness exists enacted.

Be that as it may, there can be no doubt that this new atmosphere, with its renewal of the claims of synthesis in the face of mechanistic associationism, contributed greatly to the development of Ribot, founder of the psychology of synthesis. To be sure, Kantianism was not his inspiration, much less were religious interests his guide. His sole concern was to revise Taine's conception of a "scientific psychology." For Ribot, science was doubtless analysis, but it was also synthesis. To reduce everything to elements is not enough. There are syntheses in nature which must be studied as such. Thus, at first glance it would seem that the point of departure of Ribot was a reflection upon the insufficiency of the method of Taine and the British psychologists. Yet this very notion of psychic synthesis—was it not borrowed from the major current of thought which was presiding at this time over a rebirth of intellectualism? The words of Ribot written in 1914 make an interesting comparison with the passage from Brochard just discussed.

> Thought is a function which was added in the course of evolution to the primary and secondary forms of knowledge: sensations, memory, association. From what preconditions could it have emerged? On this point, we dare not hazard hypotheses. One way or another, it made its appearance, it took definite shape, it developed. But since no function can become active except under the influence of stimuli appropriate to it, the existence of pure thought operating without anything to stimulate it is a priori implausible. Reduced to itself alone, thought is an activity that dissociates, associates, apprehends relations, coordinates. We may even suppose that this activity is by its very nature unconscious, assuming a conscious form only by way of the data which it elaborates. . . . To conclude, the hypothesis of pure thought without images and without words is most unlikely, and in any case unproven.[18]

One might be reading the very words of Brochard, couched now in biological and pragmatic language. Like Brochard, Ribot claimed the existence of sensations and images bound together by laws of association. These are "the primary and secondary forms of knowledge." Like Brochard, Ribot made these the immediate data of introspection. As for thought, he too considered it inaccessible to intuitive awareness. But for Brochard thought fails to reveal itself to intuition because it is "potential," a functional equivalence of widely differing images. Ribot, on the other hand, spoke in firmly "thingish" terms. Thought is a real activity, but unconscious. "It assumes a conscious form only by virtue of the experiential data which it elaborates." And, content with this obscure and contradictory notion of unconscious thought, this positivistic psychologist concluded a priori that the notion of pure thought accessible to consciousness is implausible. We can see how profound was the influence of Taine, forceful to the point of causing an experimental psychologist to deny experimental results in the name of pure deduction.[19] For this entire generation, associationism was to remain the factual datum, and thought was to be merely a hypothesis needed to explain "organization," to explain systematization too difficult to account for by pure association. And the objectivism [20] of Ribot, instead of applying itself to a description of the image as such, proceeded in contradiction to itself by inventing a biological notion of unconscious thought "appearing" in the course of human evolution.

The true import of this notion of "synthesis," by which Ribot differs from Taine, is apparent. It is a physiological conception. Man is a living organism enfolded in the world, and thought is an organ developed by certain needs. Just as there is no digestion without food, so there is no thought without images, that is, without materials from the outside. But just as advances in physiology led to a conception of digestion as a functional whole, so the new psychology was to reconstitute, from the raw or elaborated materials which are conscious, the synthetic unity of an organism that elaborates them. And just as synthetic psychology does not exclude determinism, so the new psychology, viewing the psychic activity of synthesis as a biological function, was to be resolutely deterministic. Thus we rediscover here the Leibnizian theme of the inseparability of thought and image, but deposed, demoted to the level of the merely thinglike. Man is a thing alive; an image is a thing; and a thought, likewise, is a thing.

Nothing conveys this dethronement better than a book by Ribot on creative imagination, *L'Imagination créatrice*. In this work he attempted to analyze the mechanism by which new images are created. Naturally, however, he put the problem in the very terms Taine would have used, asking how new groupings, or "fictions," can be constituted from images supplied by memory. And, to be sure, he began by declaring the rights of synthesis: "Every imaginative creation requires a principle of unity." But this principle which he called, without much regard for consistency, "a center of attraction and point of support," and which he conceived as a "fixated emotion-idea" [*une idée-émotion fixe*], was finally to serve simply as a regulator for merely mechanical processes. To start with, there would occur dissociation. The image of the external object would undergo a process of dismemberment. The causes of dissociation are "internal and external." The former or "subjective" causes are, first, selection in the light of action to be taken; second, affective causes "governing attention"; and third, intellectual reasons, "indicating by this term the mental law of inertia or the law of least effort."[21] The external causes are the "variations of experience," which present a certain object now with and now without a certain property, "that which has been associated now with one thing, now with another, tending to dissociate itself from both." Dissociation frees a certain number of image factors which can then associate to form new groupings. We come to the second part of the problem: "What are the forms of association that give rise to new combinations, and under what influence are they formed?"[22] We have seen that Ribot formulated this influence in associational terms. Associations may be oriented or directed from the outside, but only a miracle could suspend their laws, as only a miracle could suspend the law of gravity. In sum, just as certain economists have proposed to replace by a guided economy the economic liberalism preached by British empiricists, so we may say that Ribot replaced the free associationism of Taine and Mill by a *guided associationism*.

For creative association there are three factors: an "intellectual" factor, an "affective" factor, and an "unconscious" factor. The intellectual factor is "the faculty of thinking by analogy, meaning by analogy an imperfect sort of resemblance; similarity is a genus of which analogy is a species." Regarding the affective or emotional factor, Ribot said little in *L'Imagination créatrice,* but returned to the subject in *Logique des sentiments* [*The Logic of Feelings*].[23] First there occurs what psychoanalysts have since termed "condensation." "States of consciousness combine because they have a common affective meaning." Transfer must also be noted.

> When an intellectual state has been accompanied by a lively emotion, a similar or analogous state tends to arouse the same emotion. . . . When intellectual states have coexisted, the emotion connected to the initial state, if lively, tends to be transferred to the other states.

Thus, there may be condensation, then transfer, then condensation once more; and in this twofold rhythm, image-elements that had no primordial relationship are brought together and fused into a new grouping. As for the unconscious factor, it is no different in character from the preceding factors. It is intellectual or affective, but not directly accessible to consciousness.

To tell the truth, it was inevitable that Ribot should resort to an unconscious, for none of the factors envisaged by him appear to consciousness. We never have a consciousness of dissociation, nor of new combinations. Images suddenly emerge and present themselves immediately as what they are. Hence it was necessary to suppose that all the work was done outside consciousness. Neither associations nor synthetic factors appear to us. This entire creative mechanism is sheer hypothesis. Ribot was no more concerned to describe the facts than Taine was. He began with explanations. The psychology of synthesis, therefore, remained at the outset speculative, like analytical psychology. It confined itself merely to complicating abstract deductions by adding a factor to the combinations, attempting to erect a psychology on the model of biology, as the other psychology attempted to proceed according to the model provided by physics. As for the image, it remained for Ribot exactly what it was for Taine. For a long time, there was to be no change.

CHAPTER IV

Bergson

At the close of the century there occurred what it has become customary to call a philosophical revolution. In two works published in succession, in 1889 and in 1896, *Essai sur les données immédiates de la conscience* (Time and Free Will) and *Matière et mémoire* (Matter and Memory), Henri Bergson set himself up as a determined opponent of associationism. The classical conception of aphasia and of cerebral localizations could not hold up against criticism. A memory-image is something other and more than a mere cerebral resuscitation. The brain could not have a function of stocking images. Perception is a direct contact with the thing. Finally, the notion of psychic synthesis introduced by Ribot was to be radically transformed. Synthesis is not a mere regulative factor, for all of consciousness is synthesis, the very mode of psychic existence. In the flux of consciousness there are not solid fragments, no juxtapositions of states. Rather, inner life presents itself as an interpenetrative multiplicity [*une multiplicité d'interpénétration*]: it *endures.*[1]

All these notable pronouncements seemed to call for

an overhauling of the psychology of images, viz., the articles by Quercy, "Sur une théorie bergsonienne de l'imagination" [2] ["On a Bergsonian Theory of Imagination"], and by Chevalier and Bouyer, "De l'image à l'hallucination" [3] ["From Image to Hallucination"]. Yet a careful examination of the ideas of Bergson will reveal, despite his use of a new terminology, the problem of the image in its classical guise, and a solution that offers absolutely nothing new.

Bergson was far from conceiving the problem purely as a psychologist. In his theory of images we find his entire metaphysics, and if we would understand the role he assigns the image in the life of the mind, we must first subject to critical examination his metaphysical point of departure.

Like the empiricists he was combating, like Hume, and like the Neo-Realists, Bergson made the universe into a world of images. Every reality has an affiliation with consciousness, is analogous to consciousness or in relationship to it. Hence, we are surrounded by "images." But whereas Hume reserved the term "image" for things insofar as they are perceived, Bergson applied it to every sort of reality. Not only is the object of actual knowledge an image, but so is every possible object of a representation. "An image can be without being perceived; it can be present without being represented." [4] Representation adds nothing to the image, gives it nothing extra, no new character. The representation already exists virtual and neutralized in the image, before being a conscious representation. In order to exist actually, the representation must be isolable from the images that are reacting with it. "Instead of remaining encased in its surroundings like a thing, it stands out from them like a painting."[5] Thus, it was no longer necessary to distinguish, as Descartes did, between the thing and its image, and then to determine how a relation may be established between these two beings; nor, like Berkeley, to reduce the reality of the thing to that of the image of which we are aware; nor to retain with Hume the possibility of a reality existing in itself even though only images are known. In Bergson's realism, the thing *is* the image, and matter is the ensemble of images. "Being and being consciously perceived is not a difference affecting the nature of images, but only a difference of degree." This amounts to saying that everything is first given as participating in consciousness, or rather *as consciousness*. Otherwise no reality could ever *become* conscious, could ever take on a character alien to its very nature. Bergson was not of the opinion that consciousness must have a correlate, or, to speak like Husserl, that a consciousness is always consciousness *of* something.[6] Consciousness, for Bergson, seems to be a kind of quality, a character simply given; very nearly, a sort of substantial form of reality. It cannot arise where it is not, it cannot begin or cease to be. What is more, it can be in a purely virtual state, unaccompanied by an act or by any manifestation whatsoever of its presence. "The unconscious," Bergson was to dub this reality endowed with a secret quality. Yet this unconscious is of exactly the same nature as consciousness. There was no nonconscious for Bergson, but only a consciousness unaware of itself. There is no illuminated object blocking and receiving light. There is a pure light, a phosphorescence, and no illuminated matter. But this pure light diffused on all sides becomes actual only by reflecting off certain surfaces which serve simultaneously as the screen for other luminous zones. We have here a sort of reversal of the classic analogy: instead of consciousness being a light going from the subject to the thing, it is a luminosity which goes from the thing to the subject.[7]

The body is the center, at once reflecting and darkening, that makes an actuality of virtual consciousness, transforming certain images into actual representations by isolating them. How is this transition possible? There is no need to derive consciousness, Bergson said, since to posit the material world is to have a collection of images. There is no question of getting consciousness out of things if a thing is already consciousness in its very existence. But by a change of terminology Bergson did not, as he thought, eliminate the problem. We still need to know how to pass from unconscious image to conscious image, from the virtual to the actual. Is it conceivable that to separate an image from the rest it is enough to endow it all of a sudden with the transparency, the existence for itself, which makes it consciousness? Or, if it be maintained that the transparency was already there, can we suppose that it existed neither for itself nor for any subject whatsoever? Bergson considered negligible this characteristic, essential to the occurrence of consciousness, of appearing to itself as conscious. Confusing consciousness and the world, treating consciousness as a quasi-substantial quality, he also reduced psychological awareness to nothing more than a sort of epiphenomenon, describable in its appearances but quite inexplicable. In particular, we may ask how this unconscious, impersonal consciousness becomes the conscious consciousness of an individual subject. How do virtually represented images suddenly manage to encompass an "I" by becoming "present"? Bergson failed to tell us. Yet the whole theory of memory is based upon the existence of such a subject and on its ability to appropriate and preserve certain images.

The body functions as a selective instrument, by which an image becomes a perception. The perception is the image "brought into relation with the possible action of a certain determinate image," namely the body. But how does this relationship make a subject appear who calls this body "my body," and the other representations "my representations"? "Give me images at large," declared Bergson, "and my body is bound to cut a distinct figure among them, because they are always in flux while it remains unchanging." The solution is tempting. Motion and immobility certainly do individualize matter, to speak like Descartes, or "images," to speak like Bergson. But they certainly leave nature physical. The image remains an image. The immobile does not become "centered," that is to say, an acting "center" does not appear; above all, action, being only an image, fails to generate a subject who "refers the actions to himself."

Doubtless this was not exactly what Bergson means. Present among the images one must conceive a mind [*un esprit*] which defines itself in terms of a memory. Gathering images, this mind makes comparisons and syntheses, and distinguishes *its* body from images surrounding it. "Once perceived, images are fixed and located in memory." But now we are thrown into the center of insoluble difficulties. To begin with, if all is consciousness, what could *a* consciousness be? Activity and unity? shall we say. A reality distinct from the rest and capable of achieving awareness [*capable de prendre conscience*]? [8] In that case, one could scarcely term "consciousness" the passive realities which consciousness can apprehend, and one would come back to a metaphysics taking its point of departure from a consciousness[9] facing a world, rather than from the world as conscious. Is consciousness rendered individual by its content, which is selected by the body to which it is joined? In that case, we can no longer understand how the body itself (together with the images related to it) manages to distinguish itself from other bodies with their surrounding images, for the relations of action between the body-image and the other images are themselves images. Yet this second conception was to be espoused by Bergson.

Another difficulty arises. How does an image turn itself into a memory-image? The image is after all a *thing* isolated by the body and granted through such isolation the new quality of being represented. But when the action of the body ceases, how can the image remain isolated and preserve its representative character? Since this table regains all its relationships with all the other images in the universe as soon as I stop looking at it, it should then become once more a virtually conscious table. How, then, can it remain at the same time a table in my memory? Or should we not say that representation is determined not merely by the isolating of the image, but appears as a reality radically distinct from any *thing?* The transition from the first to the second chapter of *Matière et Mémoire* is managed by a pure sophism. The representative image is first an image ideally isolated and actually linked to all the others; then, as it becomes a memory-image, it detaches itself from the world and transforms itself in the mind, the ideal isolation turning into a real isolation. Bergson was misled by his physical terminology in comparing an image and a picture—as a man who isolates a bit of landscape by looking at it through a spyglass, and then proposes to carry off not only the spyglass but also the bit of landscape framed by it. The entire Bergsonian theory of images is based on a sophism which accounts for its realist character. Memory carries off the picture-image exactly as one may cart away a painting one has unhooked from the wall. Memory "keeps gathering images as they occur." Bergson did not overlook the fact that picture-images are also thing-images, encased in other images and existing without being perceived; indeed, he endowed memory-images with all the plenitude of objects. More precisely, the memory-image is thus contemporaneous with the formation of the perception. The image-thing turns into a memory by becoming a representation at the moment of perception.

> The formation of a memory is never posterior to that of a perception, but contemporaneous with it. As a perception arises, the memory is adumbrated alongside.[10]

Thus constituted, the memory

> is at once perfected. Time could add nothing to its image without denaturing it. It will retain for memory its place and its date.[11]

This conception of images advanced by Bergson was far from being as different from the empiricist conception as he claimed. For Bergson as for Hume an image is an element of thought exactly fitting the perception: the same discontinuity, the same individuality of character. For Hume, the image appeared as a weakening of the perception, an echo subsequent to it in time; for Bergson, it was a shadow paired with the perception.

In both cases, the image was an exact decalcomania of the thing: opaque, impenetrable like the thing, rigid, frozen, in fine, itself a thing. "Indeed, images are never anything but things." This is the explanation for the considerable resemblance which we shall note between the role of the image in the mind according to Bergson and its role according to the empiricists. For Bergson too the image was first characterized as "imprinting" itself in the mind, like a content for which memory is only a receptacle, rather than a living feature of mental activity.

Yet Bergson laid particular stress on having established a difference in kind, not merely in degree, between perception and memory, in contrast to the empiricists. But this very distinction, more metaphysical than psychological, was to raise new problems. We have already noted it: a perception is an image brought into relation with possible bodily action, yet still encased among the other images, and a memory is the image isolated, set apart from the others like a painting. Everything real has at one and the same time the two characteristics of disposing the body to action and of depositing itself in the mind as an inoperative memory.

> **In its very upsurge, the present duplicates itself each moment into two symmetrical sprays, one of which falls back into the past, the other of which propels itself toward the future.**[12]

Thus a profound difference exists between memory, inactive, a mere idea, and perception, an ideo-motor activity. However, not only would we be unable to discriminate by this distinction between the perception and the *actualized* memory (the *re*appearing image of the table), but what is meant by this perpetual doubling of the present is perfectly incomprehensible; just as, earlier, we were unable to conceive how a provisional isolation of the thing would suddenly make it a representation. The same fundamental sophism is betrayed by the metaphor of a double spray. Indeed, what can the present be? "My present is, in essence, sensori-motor." It is a "cut" effected by perception in a flowing mass. This cut is precisely "the material world," "a thing which is absolutely determinate and which stands forth from the past."

It is glaringly evident that such a definition of the present is metaphysically inadequate, and involves a vicious circle, since a pragmatic present requires for its possibility an ontological present. But criticism along these lines exceeds the limits of our topic. Let us accept the definition as given. We cannot help but observe immediately that a present which is *pure activity* could not by doubling itself produce an inoperative past, a pure idea disconnected from movements and sensations. Consider either the action-memory relation in the subject or the image-thing relation in the object: there appears the same hiatus between two kinds of existence that Bergson was anxious to posit as distinct (since he wished to separate mind from matter, memory from body), but that he nonetheless wished to bring into a unity. To justify these two contradictory undertakings he resorted to a syncretic mixture of consciousness and matter. Having repeatedly confused noema and noesis [13] he was led to give this syncretic reality, called an "image," now the status of a noema, now a noetic status, according to the demands of his theoretical structure. Of unification, there was none; only a constant, a perpetual slipping without good faith from one realm to the other. Thus did Bergson try to explain what empiricists regard as a given: the existence of images born of perception. We have seen that he failed. But the position he took forced him to resolve another problem, namely, how an image can reinsert itself into the sensori-motor world of body and of perception. How can the past become the present all over again?

The true home of the picture-image is memory. Like thing-images, it can be conscious actually or—what amounts in this case to a condition of unconsciousness—virtually. Now, since the overwhelming majority of our memories are unconscious, one must ask how they return to consciousness. Bergson answered this question with two theories that were irreconcilable, yet were not sharply distinguished. One had its roots in the psychologism and biologism of Bergsonian thought; the other, in its metaphysics, its tendencies toward mentalistic interpretations [*spiritualisme*]. The first theory seems clear enough at first: the actual is the present, and the present is delineated by the action of the body. To evoke a memory is to render present a past image. But the evoked image is not a mere revival of the stored image, otherwise one could never understand how, with respect to a multitude of distinct memories corresponding to a multiplicity of perceptions, I can evoke an unique image which may well fail to coincide exactly with any of the recorded memories. To return to consciousness the image must insert itself in the body. In the body and its motor mechanisms the psychological, conscious image is an incarnation of the pure, inoperative, and unperceived memory that existed in the unconscious. Living, for the mind, is always "to insert itself among things by way of some mechanism." Such is the condition of a memory. In its pure state it is "fixed, precise, but . . . lifeless." It is virtual, impotent, like those souls of which Plato spoke, that must let themselves fall into a body in order to become actual. Thus, to become present a memory has to insert itself into a bodily posture. Summoned from the depths of memory, a recollection becomes an operative reality, an image, by developing in memory-images that insert themselves into some bodily posture. Hence Bergson could write: "An image is a present state and can participate in the past only by means of the memory from which it emerged." Bergson insisted on the role of movement, pointing out that every image (visual, auditory, etc.) is always accompanied by schematic motor activities. On this theory, an image should appear as a construction in the present, an awareness of a standpoint defined in the present by movements of the body. Two consequences are bound to follow. First, nothing would distinguish an image from a perception, which is likewise a present viewpoint, and the image would be, like the perception, a doing rather than a knowing. Second, an image would not be a memory but a new creation in response to the ceaseless novelties of the postures of the body.

But if consciousness was defined by Bergson in vitalistic terms, as an actuality resulting from the bodily state, it also meant to him the margin between action and agent, the capacity to escape the present and the body, in short, memory. There resulted the second of his two theories. A recollection is not only conscious as present but as already past. In his essay already cited, "Le Souvenir du Présent," Bergson acknowledged, as we have seen, that at the very moment of perceiving an object we may have a memory of it, from which results the phenomenon known as paramnesia. Obviously the memory in its actuality is not determined in this case by the body, since a representation born of a bodily stance before an object is termed a "perception." The recollection has an awareness *sui generis* enabling it *to be present as a memory,* whereas a perception *is present as a perception.* The body, in that case, instead of seeming to be of use to memory in a positive fashion, merely must not keep the recollection from appearing. Instead of an insertion of the recollection into the body, there must be a suppression of the body, so to speak, as in the lowering of the tension of the nervous system during sleep. Dreams and hypermnemonic phenomena show what a wealth of imagery may accompany such physiological annihilation.

But if consciousness is, according to this second theory, directly connected with the mind, the power of the body to turn consciousness away from the mind and make it subscribe to action becomes inconceivable. One cannot find the slightest reason why memory-images should not be conscious at all times. This explains, as we indicated earlier, why Bergson held two theories simultaneously. The body makes the memory into an actuality, into clear awareness, yet memory makes perception, a mere schema of motor activity, into a conscious representation. Just how, then, does this meeting take place?

The schema of motor activity is generated by perception, by present action, but memories are introduced by some sort of force belonging to memory itself. Thus, although memory is actionless, Bergson endowed it with tendencies or powers no less magical than the attractive powers attributed to images by Hume. According to

Bergson, images try "to struggle into the light," and an effort is required "to inhibit their appearance." As soon as the pressure is relaxed, "the motionless memories, sensing that I have removed the obstacles to raising the trapdoor which kept them in the cellar of consciousness, begin to move." Only by a veritable effort does the body block the appearance of the totality of memories that otherwise would come into existence, and in principle could do so. Such metaphors are, at the very least, unfortunately chosen. What now becomes of the role of screening and reflecting assigned as fundamental to the body? And what of the notable definition, "The unconscious is the inactive," which Bergson seemed to have quite forgotten while describing at length the "dance" engaged in by memories?

Moreover, whence do memories acquire an appetite for actual existence? The past, Bergson held, is at least as real as the present, which is but a limit. An unconscious representation exists as fully as a conscious one. Whence, then, this desire to incarnate itself in a body both alien in character and unnecessary to its existence? Why are memories "on the lookout . . . , almost paying attention," instead of being inert or indifferent? Speaking more generally, to attribute an activity of a mental sort to discontinuous elements, to contents of consciousness first carefully severed from the whole of consciousness, is to leave oneself open to the intervention of material forces of a magical sort that prove to be completely inconceivable.

Nor is the nature of the appeal "launched" to memory by perception any clearer. Perception is not a representation but a schema of motor activity, which undertakes to constitute the image that attaches to the perception.

But once again we may ask why perception, by nature action rather than speculation, strives to turn itself into a representation. Above all, if the perception is not a representation, if the memory is but an exact decalcomania of the perception, a shadow of perception, *where does the representation come from?* "Memory," wrote Bergson, "makes us see and hear. Perception is incapable of evoking the matching memory." Indeed, the perception would already have had to take form, a form that must come from memory. Perception is an image annexed to a certain bodily posture which is at first fairly general, corresponding only to the most external characteristics of the object. Depth and meaning are furnished by memory. But nowhere did Bergson say where the initial meaning and form come from. Moreover, Bergson explained at length in *Matière et mémoire* that "to perceive is to remember" (taking "perception" in the sense of representation in the present, not in the pure sense). But then there are only two alternatives: either the image does not bear within itself the mark of its past origin and gives itself as one with the present, contrary to an earlier claim by Bergson, or else perception necessarily gives itself as an image arriving from the past. Once again, no real difference is evident between a memory-image, which is a fragment of the past incarnated in a present motor schema [*schème moteur*], and a perception, which is a present motor schema incarnating a past memory. Despite every effort, Bergson failed to distinguish them, and we discover beneath these specious theories the plain statement of the empiricists that an image and a perception differ only in degree, not in kind. Thus, after having carefully distinguished images and perceptions on the metaphysical level, Bergson was forced to confound the distinction on the psychological level.

It remained to be seen what role this memory-image was to play in the life of the mind. We have already noted that Bergson was led to an associationist conception, because for him, as for the associationists, an image is a solidified element, a thing. To be sure, Bergson fought strenuously against the associationist view. But he failed to realize that associationism must always have the best of it with those who concede that an image is a thing, even if the mind is reinstated face to face with the thing. He failed to see that the only way to be rid of this intrusive doctrine is to come back to the image itself and to demonstrate that it is radically different from a thing. He limbered up the concept of consciousness, attempting to give it fluidity, spontaneity, life. But to no avail, for he left inert images at the heart of pure duration, like tiles at the bottom of a pool. One must begin all over again.

This is not to say that Bergson's works contained no cogent critique of associationism. He attacked first the notions of resemblance and contiguity conceived as gentle forces. Images as such, he asserted, do not possess a mysterious power of attracting each other. Their connections arise from the action into which they insert themselves, in short, from the body. Every perception spreads out in motor reactions utilizing motor mechanisms established by analogous perception, and these reactions involve other reactions previously co-ordinated to them, and so on. Thus are provided the links of resemblance and contiguity, which may be traced back to mechanical connections in the body, to bodily memory or memory as habit. Similarly, a general idea is not the result of a superimposition of individual images. Lived before being thought, general ideas are precisely over-all reactions to total situations, and their generality lies in the similarity of the reactions to various situations. Thus, the mind does not first form images which unite later to yield concepts and particular connections. Rather, perception provides syntheses only subsequently dispersed into images.

> **Consequently, association is not the primary fact. Dissociation is first, and the tendency of every memory to annex others must be explained by a natural return of the mind to the undivided unity of perception.[14]**

But how can this fragmenting occur? The question is an important one, for Bergson conceived the mind as oscillating between two poles, that of synthetic perception, which defines the present, and that at which images are spread out externally to each other. Understanding, fancying, remembering, hence thinking in general, always involve passing from one pole to the other by way of intermediate stages less concentrated than the first and less dispersed than the second. The mind lives, not by reassembling separate elements, but by contracting or dilating a synthetic content always given in its totality. What, then, is the origin of these different levels of consciousness? In particular, how can the level of the past, of a dream, emerge from the level of action? In these accounts the relation of image to perception is quite different from the account given earlier. The image duplicated the perception like a shadow; indeed, an image was said to be the perception itself fallen into the past, the image-thing simply isolated from its surroundings so as to become a picture-image. Now, on the contrary, perception seems to contain synthetically a multitude of images, which the tension of the body endows with an undivided unity, and which scatter as soon as the body lets go.

The trouble, as we have seen, is that the role of the image in perception has not been made clear. We do not know the origin, for Bergson, of the primary representations. Into every complex perception are inserted a multitude of images springing from the unconscious and constituting at one and the same time the perceptual image and the memory image. In a certain sense, then, there is indeed a multiplicity of images in *a* perception. But if one considers the perceptual image an undivided unity, the new memory image corresponding to it must also be considered a unity. Inversely, if the latter is considered a composite, the perception must itself be considered a composite. The strongest reasons require that the primary images be exactly the same in their concentration and content as the primary perceptions.

Further, what could Bergson have meant by the notions of fragmentation, externality, and dissociation, having proved so conclusively that the life of the mind cannot be expressed by spatial metaphors? If he was led to introduce them anyway, this was because, on the one hand, he knew perfectly well that consciousness is at all times a unity, but on the other hand his realist theory of memory obliged him to attribute to unconscious objects precisely the discontinuity and multiplicity characteristic of objects in the physical world. Since his metaphysics demanded that this storehouse of isolated images be really present in the mind at all times, consciousness must diversify itself only by means of the various kinds of unity which it assigns to this multifarious reality. Hence the comparison to a gas in different degrees of tension, such that the same number of molecules can be contained in different volumes; hence, also, the theory of different levels of consciousness. But the notion of synthesis so dear to Bergson was still conceived in an extremely materialistic fashion. No doubt, instead of the traditional juxtaposition, he suggested a fusion of elements; but the notion of elements remained. Bergson tried to replace the geometrical and spatial conceptions of Cartesianism and the associationists with a mentalistic conception [*un spiritualisme*]. He generated only a physicochemical fairy tale many of whose relationships are prelogical. What, indeed, could be meant by such "fusion"? The "fusion" of molecules in the kinetic theory of gases? The elements of a gas may take up different volumes, for the spaces between them may be reduced, but the molecules could not be made to interpenetrate. By what warrant, then, are these psychic molecules, these Bergsonian images, supposed to blend into a unifying synthesis. Shall we say that such a synthesis is peculiar to consciousness? But once a realist metaphysics of memory has been constructed, one cannot attribute any such power *sui generis* to the psychic. The image remains a thing, a solidified element; grouped with other images, only a mosaic could result. Thus, when the mind functions at any level of consciousness, only mechanical connections occur, just as described by associationism. Bergson even referred to a whole region of psychic life, that of dreams and daydreams, as inferior or mechanical, involving purely associative connections among images.

The spontaneity of mind lay in the possibility of passing from one level to another, by means of what Bergson called "the dynamic schema." This is a unity, a synthesis containing the rules for a development into images, "an indication of what must be done to reconstitute images." "It contains in a state of reciprocal implication *what the image is to develop as parts external to each other.*" [15]

If memory is allowed to wander, the images, homogeneous, will follow each other on the same level of consciousness. But one may, instead, "transport oneself to a point at which the multiplicity of images seems to condense into a unique, simple, indivisible representation." In this case, recollection would consist merely in returning once more from the schema [16] to the level at which the images are scattered. To understand, to recollect, to feign is always to form a schema first, and then, descending once more from the schema to the image, to fill the schema with images, this process of realization perhaps yielding a modification of the schema. Thus would be explained the unity and organization of mental activity impossible to account for by beginning instead with separate elements. Flexibility and novelty come from the schema. Bergson concluded: "*Besides* the associative mechanism, there is the mechanism of mental effort." No more is needed to date Bergson's thought. Might we not be reading a remark by Ribot? Bergson failed to understand any better than Ribot that one cannot come to terms with associationism. If one accepts the notions of a solidified image and mechanical connections, if one introduces into consciousness an opaqueness or resistance alien to it, a world of "things," one cannot comprehend the nature of a fact of consciousness. How is consciousness to master elements foreign to it? Or, in Bergsonian terms, how is the flexibility of the schema to adjust to the rigidity of the image? Once more, one must fall back on magic. Between schema and image, Bergson declared in very vague terms, occur "attraction" and "repulsion." But it is easy to see that he could not account for the selectiveness shown by images, their way of recognizing the schemata into which they can insert themselves.

Above all, if images can yield only "mosaics," how can the schema modify them to the point that they blend into a new image irreducible in character? In short, how explain creative imagination? When all is said and done, the schema acts merely as a catalyst, differing very little from "the principle of unity, the center of attraction and point of support" whose existence was posited by Ribot. *Before,* only separate images can be found; *afterward,* images are grouped interdependently in a new order. But no "gentle force" directly ordering images about and emanating from them without intermediaries could be any more mysterious in producing the same results. The alternative would be to concede that the schema modifies the internal structure of the image. But this would presuppose an entirely different theory by which an image would appear to be an *act* rather than a content, the schema, in consequence, playing no role whatsoever.

Bergson failed to provide a satisfactory solution to the problem of images. He did no more than place one level of psychological life on another, insisting on the rights of the notions of synthesis and continuity. The psychology of images he neither touched upon, nor enriched with a single new insight. He never *looked at* his images. Despite repeated appeals to concrete intuition, it was all dialectic, a priori deduction. Into the metaphysics of Bergson passed Taine's "image," unexamined and whole.

And the world of thought that Bergson tried unsuccessfully to reinstate was irremediably cut off from the world of images and from a host of resources.

It should be added that Bergson frequently hesitated over this issue and that, in some lectures, he attributed to images a function incompatible with their nature as given in *Matière et mémoire* and *L'Énergie spirituelle*. For example, in "L'Intuition philosophique" ["Philosophical Intuition"] he regarded the image as "intermediate between the simplicity of concrete intuition and the complexity of the abstractions into which it is translated," and showed the need for resorting to this mediating term, "almost matter in that it may still be seen and almost mind in that it cannot be touched." The solidified, the spatial, the fragmentary, these now appeared as marks of the concept, and the image was more condensed and nearer to intuition. "A system develops into concepts, and condenses into an image when urged back toward the intuition from which it was derived." Thus, whenever Bergson mentioned intuition he tended, in distrust of discursive thought, to reappraise images at high value. But his theory of a dynamic schema, by sanctioning an impossibility of passing from reproductive imagination to creative imagination, removed the very means of relating this philosophical function of the image to its psychological nature.

CHAPTER V

Bergsonism

We have witnessed the failure of Bergson's attempt to provide a new solution to the problem of images. But we must recognize that Bergson was not the whole of "Bergsonism." He generated a certain atmosphere, a way of seeing, a tendency always to look for the moving, the living. In this methodological aspect, so to speak, Bergsonism represented a main current of prewar thought.[1] The chief characteristic of this state of mind seems to us to have been an optimism at once superficial and lacking in good faith. A problem was supposed to have been resolved when the terms had been dissolved in an amorphous continuity. We might conjecture, therefore, that Bergsonians differing from Bergson in their treatment of the question of images would endow the image with a malleability and a mobility denied by the master.

Thus Spaier tried to show, in early writings [2] explicitly referring to Bergsonian thought, that images live. They are born and they die, they have their "dawn" and their "dusk," they grow and develop. For associationism an image was in action or it was nothing at all. For the Bergsonians an image was to be a passage from potency to act, like motion in Aristotle. An image develops and proceeds toward actualization and complete individualization, that is, toward an existence like that of an individualized *thing*. Its status in associationism was merely the ideal culmination of its development. But this development may be arrested in its course. Subjects remarked on a tendency of thought to save its energy, the full comprehension of an idea preceding the complete disappearance of the image. In this case, the image vanished without realizing its possibilities to the full. We could not even know what it would have been at the limit of actualization. For the associationists the passage from one image to another involved two steps: a pure and simple annihilation of the first, then a creation *ex nihilo* of the second. They succeeded each other without touching, like two phenomena connected by a causal relation in Hume. The Bergsonian psychologists reinstated a transitive causality between successive images. One might even speak of continuous transformations of a single image, where classical psychology would have seen a succession of discontinuous appearances. Thus the image was promoted from the mineral to the living realm. Each image developed according to its own laws. The mechanical causality of Hume and Taine, which assumed the inertia of the related elements, was to be replaced by a biological determinism. An image was a living form, a relatively autonomous life in the whole psychic life. These metaphors were supposed to have rendered the image homogeneous with thought.

At the same time, the notion of a schema [3] was riding high. Psychologists and linguists were to make a habit of using this abridged image midway between a pure individual sense-datum and a pure thought. To be sure, the schema was not derived solely from Bergsonism. Such thinkers as Baldwin and Revault d'Allonnes underwent many other influences before setting forth their psychology of schemata. But the schema found in Bergsonism a favorable soil for growth. It, too, was a potentiality. Thought in potency, image in potency, it retained the role of an intermediary [4] which it already had in Kant and which Bergson had preserved. In fact, this was the only point on which its supporters were in agreement. The schema was agreed to have, like the "daemon" of Platonic philosophy, a mediating function. It established continuity between two types of existence which were irreconcilable at their farthest reaches, surmounting and resolving in itself the conflicts of image and thought. But just because of this mixed character, this conciliatory synthesis, there was much uncertainty regarding its nature. Now it was thought to be a unifying principle loaded with sensory matter; now an impoverished image, a skeleton; and now an original image, a pure determination of geometrical space supposedly translating ideal relationships into spatial ones.

Making images more malleable and creating a schema —is this progress toward the concrete? We think not. We think, rather, that these new theories were all the more dangerous for having appeared to be a new formulation of the issue, whereas in fact they merely perfected and brought up to date the old associationist mistake. The image, it was said, is *living*. But what did that mean? Is it simply a phase of the life of consciousness as a whole, or is it only *a* life *in* consciousness? One need only survey the abundant Bergsonist literature on the subject to realize that the image remained *a thing in consciousness*. To begin with, the image had not lost its sensory content, nor, consequently, its status of revived sensation. It merely became more malleable. Whereas a revival of Taine's image was always the same, always a copy, the living image drew its meaning, as it reappeared, from the moment of psychic life in which it appeared. The sensory content was always there, but the form it adopted was constantly undone and redone. So it seemed enough to free the image from its past. It was indeed easier to take account in this way of the creative function of imagination, for every image is in its spontaneity and unpredictability a creation. But was the relation of form to matter made any more understandable in this psychic reality termed an "image"? Whence the perpetual renovation of the image, its perpetual adaptation to the present situation, if its sensory content remained the same? In consciousness, it would be replied, all is activity. Well and good—but what is meant by a sensory content that is active? A sense-datum [*un sensible*] with the property of transforming itself spontaneously? In that case, it is no longer a sense-datum. So be it, we are told, it is no longer a sense-datum. Let it suffice that there remain the irreducible *quality* of red or rough or sharp. But who can fail to see that the condition *sine qua non* of this irreducible quality is inertness, absolute passivity? Kant noted in the *Critique of Pure Reason* the radical difference between sensory intuition, which is necessarily passive, and an active intuition productive of its object.

Above all, however, the Bergsonian image is always posited as confronting a thought which deciphers it. More malleable and more mobile, no doubt, but impenetrable nonetheless. It must be *awaited*. If for any reason it were to disappear before being completely formed, we could never know what it was to have been. We must observe it, decipher it. In a word, it keeps *teaching* us something. What is this but to say that the image is a *thing?* Doubtless the heavy stones of Taine have been replaced by living, delicate mists which change ceaselessly. But for all that these mists do not cease to be things. If the image was to be made homogeneous with thought, no one should have been satisfied to make it diaphanous, changing, almost transparent. Its status as a *thing* had to come under attack. Otherwise, one is open to the criticism that although thought is fluid, diaphanous, changing, almost transparent, and although these same terms have been applied to the image, these identical terms do not have the same meanings in both usages. When you speak of the fluidity and the diaphanous character of thought, it could be charged, you are using metaphors that could not be taken literally. When you attribute the same qualities to an image, you really do attribute them, since you have made it a thing confronting thought. Your assertion of the homogeneity of thoughts and images (as you conceive images) depends on a mere play on words. Henceforth it is no use saying that an image is a living organism, for you have in any case failed to cancel out its status of a thing. You have not freed it from the laws of association, just as the fact of being alive does not free an organism from the law of gravity.

As for schemata, they merely represent an attempt at reconciling two extremes. But the very fact of using this notion clearly shows that one continues to assert these extremes. Without thing-images there would be no need for schemata. In Kant and in Bergson the schema was never more than a contraption to link the activity and unity of thought to the inert multiplicity of the sensory. The schematic solution therefore appeared as a classic answer to a certain way of formulating the question. On a different formulation, the very meaning of the schema would disappear. Do you say that you have in consciousness right now an abridged representation, too concrete to be a thought, and too indeterminate to be assimilated to the individual things surrounding us? And you call this representation a "schema"? But why would this not be simply an image? By setting up a separate classification for these abridged representations, do you not admit that you confine the term "image" to a faithful and exhaustive copy of a *thing?* But perhaps images are never copies of objects. Perhaps they are only procedures for *rendering objects present* in a certain way. In that case, what happens to the schema? It is merely an image like all the rest. For an image would not be defined by the wealth of details with which it renders an object present, but by the manner in which it eyes the object.

CHAPTER VI

The Würzburg School

As the century opened, however, the problem of the image was to undergo modifications quite different in import from the alleged Bergsonian "revolution." The Cartesian viewpoint on thing-images was due to put in an appearance again. In rapid succession, in fact, there appeared: Marbe's *Recherches de psychologie expérimentale sur le jugement* (1901), Binet's *Étude expérimentale de l'intelligence* (1903) in which his position of 1896 was completely abandoned, Ach's article "Sur l'activité volontaire de la pensée" (1905), Messer's *Recherches de psychologie expérimentale sur la pensée,* Bühler's *Faits et problèmes pour une psychologie des processus de pensée* (1907–8), Marie's *Révision de la question de l'aphasie* (1906), and somewhat later his article, "Sur la Fonction du langage," in *Revue philosophique.* Though differing greatly in character and derivation these works were to result in a rebirth of the Cartesian conception of the relation between images and thoughts.

The dilemma of Brochard, Ferri, and all the rationalists of the eighties was well-known. They had believed themselves wedged between the factual data of physiology and those of introspection. Consciousness never observes in itself anything but image-like representations, and cerebral activity is localized in character: two grand scientific principles, apparently supported inductively by an imposing quantity and variety of observations. Yet, in spite of it all, those thinkers wished to reinstate the existence of synthetic thought employing concepts, grasping relations, and regulated step by step by the laws of logic. Hence the recourse to Leibniz and the straightforward assertion of the rights of thought. But the physiological theory of cerebral localization was suddenly to lose its standing among medical men. It had been based, it seemed, on dubious material. Experience had been consulted by methods grounded in John Stuart Mill, and was worth exactly as much as those methods. Taking up the question of aphasia, from which the scientific theory of localization originated, Marie showed that there do not exist a number of disturbances each of which corresponds to a lesion of a particular center. Rather, there is only one type of aphasia, corresponding simply to a general lowering of the psychic level, and thus to a synthetic incapacity. In aphasia, it is intelligence that is disturbed. From this point on, physiology was to turn gradually toward a synthetic conception of the brain. To be sure, different regions of the organ can be distinguished as having different functions, but these cannot be reduced to a mosaic of cell groups.

At the same time, the work of the Würzburg School [1] was to transform the whole conception of the data of intuition. Subjects had found in themselves states without images. Thought had revealed itself to them without any intermediary. The existence of pure cognitions, of "consciousness of rules," of "tensions of consciousness," had been noted. As for images properly speaking, the data of inner experience provided confirmation of the Bergsonian theories. The image is supple and mobile. Objects appearing in images are not restricted to the same individuation as objects of perception.

Thought appears to itself without intermediary, thinking and to know that one is thinking are all one: such was the great innovation of the theories of Würzburg. Earlier we compared to the physicotheological argument the attempt of Leibniz and his successors to prove from the very order of images the existence of thought beyond images. Now, however, proof becomes unnecessary. As God reveals Himself to the contemplation of the mystic, so thought allows itself to be apprehended in a privileged experience. And the worth of this special experience is certified by the Cartesian *cogito*.

It is not part of our purpose to expound the works of the Würzburg School. A host of monographs on the subject are available in French, English, and German. On the worth and range of introspective experiment all that is needful has been said. We would simply like to call attention to the fact that the German psychologists did not approach experience without preconceived notions.

To tell the truth, their work did not have a purely psychological purpose. One might even say that they sought to limit rigorously the domain of psychology. Their labors were conceived under the influence of the *Logische Untersuchungen* of Husserl,[2] the first volume of which is occupied with an exhaustive critique of psychologism in all its forms. Opposing psychologism's attempt to reconstitute the life of thought by means of "contents of consciousness," Husserl set forth a new conception of a transcendent sphere of meanings, each of which is a "represented" rather than a "representation," and none of which can in any way be constituted by contents. Corresponding to this world of meanings there obviously is a special type of psychic state, that is to say, there are states of consciousness which *represent* these meanings and which may be empty intentions or more or less clear, more or less full intuitions. In any event, meaning and consciousness of meaning escape psychology. The study of meaning as such belongs to logic. The study of the consciousness of signification belongs, after a special "conversion" or "reduction," to a new discipline, phenomenology. We encounter here once again what we saw in Descartes: essences, intuitions of essences, acts of judgment, and deductions completely escape psychology, conceived as a genetic and explanatory subject passing from fact to law. Rather, psychology is itself rendered possible by essences.

Indeed, one concern of the Würzburg psychologists was none other than to confirm on grounds of introspective experiment the antipsychologism of Husserl. If Husserl was right, there must be in the course of consciousness special states which would be precisely awarenesses of meanings. And if such states exist, their essential character would be to limit psychology by setting its boundaries. They could no doubt be described and classified, and for this reason they would still be the property of psychologists. But their very existence means that we must give up attempting to explain them by showing their origins in prior contents. For they represent the way in which logic is given to human awareness.

By their discovery of pure thought the Würzburg psychologists supposed that they had proven the existence of a pure logic. This a priori conception of thinking dictated their point of view on images as the purely psychological over against the purely logical, the inert content confronting thought. Between the world of images and the world of thought yawned an abyss, the very abyss observed in Descartes. Turning to purposes of his own, the famous passage of the Meditations in which Descartes showed that the understanding alone can think a piece of wax in its true nature, Bühler wrote: "I maintain that in principle any object can be fully and accurately thought without the help of images." [3] It followed that images, for these psychologists, could only be an embarrassment for thinking, representing an inopportune reappearance of the thing in the middle of our awareness of meaning. Thus, Watt wrote that "every image appears as a hindrance (*Hemmung*) to ideational processes." The image is a left-over, a regressively oriented organ. Since an object can always be rendered present in its pure essence, the use of images is ever a waste of time and a degradation. Thus the image retained for Watt and for Bühler a detracting, *thing-like* character. They never studied it in its own right, nor did they take advantage of the rich crop of facts yielded by their experiments. Their theory of images therefore remained purely negative in character, and the image remained for them what it had been for Taine: a revival of the thing.

Whether the Würzburg psychologists really understood Husserl—whether an entirely new psychology was not rather called for by the *Logische Untersuchungen*—

we will have to decide later. For the moment it will suffice to show how the notion of pure thought, which became a settled fact of psychology despite Ribot, Titchener, and others, remained confused and unsteady. At about this time, Binet performed some experiments which revealed in his nieces some thoughts without images.[4] But he failed to consult experience freely and without preconceptions. Starting from associationism, he did not undergo the influence of the synthetic viewpoint in psychology until later. Consequently he retained almost unwittingly the old conception of images derived from Taine. His aim was to establish a thought existing *over against* images. The image immediately seemed to him a "feeble print," a penny coin over against a hundred-dollar thought. Doubtless the image was now acknowledged to enter into synthetic combinations, but only as a discrete element. Most important, however, his views were already formed, and he did not wait for experience to reveal either the existence or the nature of thought. Or rather, he hesitated between two opposed views.

Thought often appeared to him as a *fact* accessible to introspection. For example, he cited for comment the famous remark of one of his subjects, "Thought seems to be a feeling like any other." But under the influence of the biological pragmatism of the time he made it into an awareness of a bodily condition. This was tantamount to Cartesianism undercut, collapsed to the level of naturalism, just as Ribot represented the undermining of the Leibnizian view. Thus we find at the time not merely the principal metaphysical theories (reappearing, for example, in Brochard and Bühler) but projections of them on the plane of a naturalism whose belief in its own "empiricism" [5] was proportional to its crudity.

From this viewpoint, however, Binet slipped imperceptibly into another conception. Pondering like Brochard on the disparity between image and meaning, he concluded that thought *must* be something other than image. So, without leaving the naturalistic level, he betook himself to the *"de jure"* level, in this famous statement which completely contradicted his earlier descriptions: "Thought is an unconscious act of the mind which requires images and words to become conscious."

Thought thus remained real enough, the notion of *de jure* or "in principle" having been hypostatized and hardened into the notion of an unconscious. But such thought is no longer accessible to itself. If I think the statement, "I will go to the country tomorrow," the only mental accompaniment may be a vague image of a plot of grass. In this case, Binet said, the image is insufficient to render all the meaning contained in the words. So it was necessary to posit the needed complement outside consciousness, in the unconscious. But a serious confusion was present. In principle, *de jure,* the statement "I will go to the country tomorrow" is involved in an infinity.[6] To begin with, there must be a "tomorrow," that is to say, a solar system and physical and chemical constants. Furthermore, I shall have to be alive, with no serious incident shattering my family or the society in which I live. All these conditions are implicitly presupposed in this simple statement. Moreover, as Binet was right in saying, the meaning of "the country" is inexhaustible. We may add: the meaning of "I," of "go," and of "tomorrow." We need only recall the comment of Valéry that there is not one word we can comprehend if we plumb the depths.

Valéry added, however, "He who hastens, understands," which is to say, *in fact* we never get to the bottom. The inexhaustible meaning of the statement does indeed exist, but virtually and socially. It exists for the grammarian, the logician, the sociologist. But the psychologist need not concern himself with it because he will never find an equivalent, either in consciousness, or in some parlous unconscious invented to meet the situation. No doubt there may be instances in which thought tends to make explicit the full connotation of a statement. But if we find only a meager image, as in the present case, would it not be better to ask whether a meager thought might be in our mind? Better yet: all we were aware of was an image. Might not this image be after all the very form in which the thought appeared in awareness? The plot of grass was not just any plot of grass. I recognize it: it is a bit of the expanse of field which lies at the bottom of my garden. I am in the habit of going there to sit. Furthermore, it is not an anonymous section of the field, but precisely the spot I have picked to stretch out in. Indeed, will be the reply, but how do you know this, except through thought? The question conceals the assumption, however, that the image is different from and the support of the thought. In that case, it would be in the relation of a sign to a meaning. But where is the proof? Is it not a priori possible that the image, rather than a lifeless support for the thought, is the thought itself in some form? Perhaps an image is as far as possible from a sign. Perhaps that plot of grass, far from being an anonymous sketch, constitutes a precise thought. At the threshold of a study of the relations of images to thoughts, one must discard the associationist preconception which sees an image as an inert mass, and also a false conception of thought which confuses the actual and the virtual, thus introducing an infinite into the least of our thoughts. Binet never took this step. The following excerpt, written shortly before his death, shows that in the depths of his soul he remained an associationist.

> [Psychology] studies a certain number of laws which we call "mental" to contrast them with laws of external nature from which they differ; laws which properly speaking do not deserve the name "mental" because they are . . . laws of images, and images are material elements. Paradoxical as it may seem, psychology is a science of matter, of that portion of matter with the property of pre-adaptivity.[7]

CHAPTER VII

The Classical Postulate

The year 1914 thus disclosed, unaltered, the three major points of view described in our second chapter. Associationism lived on among certain tardy partisans of the theory of cerebral localization, and was latent among a host of writers who were unable to dispose of it despite every effort. The Cartesian doctrine of pure thought which is capable of replacing the image on the very terrain of imagination returned to favor through Bühler. A large number of psychologists, finally, maintained with R. P. Peillaube the compromise theory of Leibniz. Experimentalists such as Binet and the Würzburg psychologists claimed to have noted the existence of imageless thoughts. Other psychologists no less devoted to fact, such as Titchener and Ribot, denied the existence and even the possibility of such thoughts. Matters had not advanced one step beyond the time of the publication of Leibniz's reply to Locke in the New Essays.

For the point of departure had not changed. In the first place, the old conception of images had been retained. In a more subtle form, no doubt. Experiments such as those of Spaier [1] revealed, to be sure, a sort of life where, thirty years earlier, only static elements had been seen. Images have their dawn and their dusk, and change form under the gaze of consciousness. The investigations of Philippe doubtless revealed a progressive schematization of images in the unconscious.[2] Generic images were admitted to exist, the work of Messer revealing a host of indeterminate representations in consciousness, and Berkeleyan particularism was abandoned. With Bergson, Revault d'Allonnes, Betz and others the old notion of schemata came back into fashion. But there was no surrender of principle: the image was an independent psychic content capable of assisting thought but also subject to its own laws. And although a biological dynamism replaced the traditional mechanistic conception, the essence of the image continued nonetheless to be passivity. In the second place, the problem of images was always approached with the same preconceptions. It was always a matter of taking a stand on the metaphysical question of mind and body, or on the methodological question of analysis and synthesis. The mind-body problem was not always formulated, no doubt; not, at least, in the same terms. For all that, it lost none of its importance. Imagination, along with the sensory [*la sensibilité*], remained the realm of bodily passivity. When Brochard, Ferri, and Peillaube fought the associationism of Taine, trying to limit it without liquidating it, they wanted to reinstate the dignity and the rights of thought over and above the laws of the body. The center of gravity of the issue had not been shifted: to understand how matter can receive a form, how sensory passivity can be *activated* by the spontaneity of mind. At the same time, psychology was still looking for a method. Its solutions to the principal problems of imagination appeared rather as ***methodological exhibits*** than as factual results. Instead of going right to the point and shaping the method on the object, *first* method had to be defined (the analysis of Taine, the synthesis of Ribot, the experimental introspectionism of Watt, the reflective critique of Brochard, etc.), *and then applied* to the object. No one suspected that in adopting a method he was at the same time fashioning the object.

Once these premises have been accepted, there are and can be only three solutions. The validity of analysis may be asserted a priori. In this case, one asserts a methodological materialism, since one is bound to attempt to explain the higher by the lower, as Comte thoroughly demonstrated. And this materialism in method may easily be transformed into a metaphysical materialism. Or, one asserts the need to employ analysis and synthesis simultaneously, thus reinstating syntheses of thought which confront images. In this case, depending on the metaphysical position adopted, thought will represent either a mind facing a body or a biological organ facing an element. But image and thought will be given as inseparable, the former as the material support of the latter. Or else one maintains simultaneously the metaphysical rights of pure thought and the methodological rights of an unanalyzable synthesis. However, since the image remains in the guise of an inert element, the realm of pure syntheses must be restricted, yielding two types of psychic reality which coexist. There will be the inert content with its associative laws, and there will be the pure spontaneity of the mind. In this case, imaging thought and imageless thought will differ not only in kind, but also, as we saw in connection with Descartes, with respect to their *subject*. The difficulty is then to show how these subjects can amalgamate into the unity of an I.

Are we forced to choose among these three views? Having given a historical exposition of the difficulties raised by each conception, we shall now try to show that all three necessarily collapse, because all three accept as an initial postulate the rebirth of inert sensory contents.

In *La Pensée concrète* [Concrete Thinking], published in 1927, Spaier noted that experimental research on the nature of mental images had become increasingly rare after the studies of the Würzburg School. For most psychologists considered the question settled, in a manner which, here as almost everywhere, ended in eclecticism. Most indicative of the tendency to conciliate, to attenuate, to dilute was the article recently published by L. Meyerson in Dumas' *Nouveau traité de psychologie* ["New Treatise in Psychology"]. The image is still viewed as a substantive state in the flow of consciousness, but a certain mobility is acknowledged. The image lives, changes, has its dawns and its dusks. In other words, the ancient psychic "atom" was to be enhanced with the malleability given to the whole of psychic life by the notion of continuity.

> What must be admitted is that the definitive images of traditional psychology form but the very smallest part of our minds as they actually live. The traditional psychology talks like one who should say a river consists of nothing but pailsful, spoonsful, quartpotsful, barrelsful, and other moulded forms of water. Even were the pails and the pots all actually standing in the stream, still between them the free water would continue to flow.[3]

An autonomous structure known as an image was posited opposite thought, but it was granted that thinking thoroughly penetrates the image, for an image, it was said, *must be understood*.

> **Our consciousness of the idea [i.e., the image] involves our consciousness (more or less explicitly) of its meaning, and the ideas with which Psychology deals are not mere signs without signification. In other words, ideas are understood, and . . . in ordinary thinking our attention is not directed always or even mainly to the ideas, but primarily to their meanings.[4]**

Similarly Spaier wrote:

> **Most of the time our attention is not directed to the object of sensory intuition (the image or the perception), but to the meaning.[5]**

There was no notion of denying the sensory structure of the image, but only of insisting on the fact that it is already *elaborated* by thought. Elaboration, in turn, was conceived in the old form of "fragmentation" and "recombination," that is, as a combination of material elements. A type of connection was posited which was peculiar to images and quite similar to association, for it remained mechanical. But it was given less and less place, and there was rejoicing when one could write, "Here is yet another region that eludes association," [6] as if the psychologist's function were to win from association new lands, to reclaim swamps.

Thus, all was restored. The plane of images and the plane of thoughts were retained, but the attempt was made to let the notion of continuity prevail. Sharp distinctions were rejected. The unity of consciousness was asserted, and this claim, by some sort of sleight-of-hand, grounded thought in the image and the image in thought, in the name of the predominance of the whole over its component elements. The upshot was many a page such as the following one, in which is rather amusingly expressed, with an air of satisfaction, a concilatory attitude, a desire to agree with everyone.

> The image thus serves as a sign . . . It has a meaning, a relation to something other than itself. It is a substitute. It has an intellectual content, and indicates a logical reality. Never wholly isolated, it is part of a system of image-signs, and thanks to this system is understood. Never completely fluid, it has enough stability, precision, form, and homogeneity of form to be compared to other images and other signs. It is a complex, the signifying and the signified, the "sensory" and the "intelligible" mingling in the image, and constituting an indissoluble whole. One may perceive various sides, surfaces, layers of meaning or details of its sensory aspects, but thus isolated a part cannot be understood without a recollection of the whole.[7] . . . The image may be more or less active. It may be a mere illustration which trails, so to speak, after thought, without aiding in the progress of thought. It may be a positive activity that orients and guides, or a negative activity that retards or stops. It is a ramp that keeps thought from losing its way, but sometimes it is also a barrier across the way. When it is flexible, plastic, mobile, it can be an effective aid to thought of no mean sort; when, on the contrary, it is too precise, too concrete, or too stable, too persistent, it halts or sidetracks thought.[8]

The viewpoint of Meyerson is shared by many a noted thinker, but the solution that satisfies them cannot withstand serious examination. As Pascal would say, the difficulties have been covered rather than removed. Generally speaking, one should distrust the modern tendency to replace the associationist atomism with a sort of amorphous continuity in which oppositions and contrasts pale and vanish. Thought, with synthetic apperception of relations, and the image of associationism are certainly incompatible. Yet what "synthetic" psychology wants to provide as an aid to thought is still the image of associationists. Only, over the mechanical connections a veil of mist is cast, namely, "duration."[9] Thought "endures," images "endure": here is a possible reconciliation. What matter if they do not "endure" in the same way? Contemporary eclecticism has tried to preserve, by means of a Bergsonian penumbra, the rationalistic nominalism of Descartes and the "experimental data" of Würzburg; and associationism, too, as the lowest form of relation; and also the Leibnizian notion of a continuity between different modes of knowledge, especially between image and idea. The existence of raw givens constituting the very matter of the image is willingly granted, but to become a part of consciousness these data, it is asserted, must be *rethought*. Thus is set up dialectically a sort of neoplatonic progression from the almost raw image, "stable, precise, concrete," to almost pure thought which proves to contain, after all, a sensory materiality of an almost indiscernible character. Beneath these vague and general accounts, the incompatibility persists; the image remains, for all that, thoroughly physical. When Meyerson tells us, for example, that an image must not be understood as it appears but for what it portrays, he thereby introduces a distinction between the true character of an image and the way in which thought grasps it. By the same token, he assimilated images to physical symbols, such as a flag, which are always *in themselves* something other (wood, cloth, etc.) than we are liable to take them for. Generally speaking, moreover, as soon as the image is considered a sign which has to be understood, the image is thereby located outside thought. A sign, after all, remains always an external, physical support for the signifying intention. Thus reappears, within a theory of image-signs which seems purely functional, the metaphysical notion of image-traces. Similarly, when Spaier allots to judgment alone the capacity to distinguish image from perception, he naturally assimilates the object as it appears in an image to the physical object of perception. For indeed, only extrinsic characteristics could provide the distinction. This image which thought deciphers, enters into, takes apart, and puts back together again may well have acquired some time ago a flexibility formerly wanting. It remains at bottom the physical image of classical philosophy. And to say that apart from its being thought the image is nothing, is to admit that a clear understanding of an image is impossible, for it is also granted that the image is something other than what we think it to be.

Instead of dissolving positions by introducing a vague theory of continuity, it would have been better to confront them directly and attempt to discern their common postulate and the inherent contradictions to which they lead. We have shown above that the postulate common to these different theories is that of the basic identity of images and perceptions. Now we shall try to show that this metaphysical postulate, whatever conclusions one manages to derive from it, necessarily leads to contradictions.

CHAPTER VIII

The Contradictory Consequences of The Classical Postulate

A. The characteristics of "the true image"

The first step of our philosophers was to identify image and perception. The second step has to manage a distinction between them. The fact of naked intuition is that there are images and perceptions, and we are quite capable of telling them apart. Consequently, the *metaphysical identification* of these psychic states is necessarily followed by an acknowledgment of the *psychological fact* that we draw a distinction between them spontaneously. Let us note immediately that there were two ways of formulating this new problem. One could ask how the psychic structure known as an "image" presents itself to reflection *as an image,* and the structure of "perception" *as a perception*. The problem is thus limited to its strictly psychological aspect, without recourse to the *objects* of perceptions and images. Perhaps this procedure would have led sooner or later to the observation that, in spite of metaphysics, there is a difference in kind between images and perceptions. But most writers viewed the question differently. They failed to ask whether psychic formations do not give themselves immediately to consciousness *for just what they are.* Rather, they took their stand on metaphysical-logical *truth,* tacitly turning the discrimination spontaneously made by any mind between image and perception into a distinction between the true and the false. Thus Taine could assert that "a perception is a true hallucination." Nor were truth and error conceived in Spinozistic fashion as intrinsic criteria. Confronting a world of images, there is a relationship to objects. Those images to which something outside corresponds were called "true" ones, or "perception"; the rest were "mental images." The conjuring trick is obvious: the data of inner experience are transformed into external relations between contents of consciousness and a world, and immediate differentiations among contents are replaced by classifications of them in terms of something else. The metaphysical theory of images, though expected in this way to fall into line with the data of psychology, never really made common cause with the latter, but rather achieved only a certain logical resemblance. Moreover, the hardest task of all remained, namely, to discover "the characteristics of the true image,"[1] on the understanding that a true image discloses no difference in kind from a false image.

Only three solutions to this problem are possible.

The first solution is that of Hume. Images and perceptions are identical but differ in intensity. Perceptions are "strong impressions," images are "feeble impressions." Hume should be credited with having acknowledged the immediacy of the differentiation of image and perception. The distinction is made of its own accord, without the need to resort to comparisons or interpretations of signs. It occurs in some sort mechanically. Of their own accord strong impressions banish feeble impressions to a lower level of being. Unfortunately, this hypothesis does not stand up to criticism. The stability, richness, and precision of perceptions do not distinguish them from images because, to begin with, these qualities have been greatly exaggerated. As Spaier reminds us in this connection:

> **Our eyes, our ears, our mouth constantly experience very confused and indistinct impressions to which we pay hardly any heed, either because of their distant origin, or because, even if of nearby origin, they lack direct connection with our behavior.[2]**

Does it follow that we make these out to be images? Furthermore, one must consider thresholds. For a sensation to cross the threshold of consciousness, it must have a minimum intensity. If such be the nature of images as well, they must possess at least that degree of intensity. But then, would we not confuse them with sensations of the same intensity? And why does not an image of an artillery shot seem to be an actual, small cracking sound? How is it that we *never* take our images for perceptions?

But sometimes we do, it will be said. For example, I may take a tree trunk for a man.[3] No doubt. But this is no confusion of image and perception. It is a false interpretation of an actual perception. There is no case (we shall return to this point later) in which an image of a man suddenly appearing in consciousness is taken for a real man actually perceived. If we could distinguish images from perceptions only by intensity, errors would occur frequently. There would even occur on occasion intermediate worlds, at twilight, for example, compounded of real sensations and images, halfway between waking life and dream. "To suppose," wrote Spaier, "that a solid certainty is a matter of strength or vivacity of impressions is simply to reinstate the *phantasia kataleptike* of the Stoics."[4] In a word, if images and perceptions do not differ in *quality* in the first place, it is hopeless to attempt to distinguish them subsequently in terms of quantity—as Taine himself well understood:

> [An image] is the sensation itself, but resultant and revived, and from whatever standpoint we consider it, we see it coincident with sensation.[5]

Consequently, one would have to abandon any attempt to set forth an intrinsic difference between a *lone* image and a *lone* sensation. There could be no immediate recognition of an image as image. Rather, the image would *first* be given to inner experience as sensation.

> There are two moments when an image is present, an affirmative one, and a negative one that limits in part what the other posited. If the image is very precise and very intense these two moments are distinct. At first, the image seems external, located at such and such a distance from us in the case of a sound or a visible object, located in the palate, the nose, the bodily members in the case of an odor sensation, a savor, a local pain or pleasure.[6]

Thus an image *by its very nature* declares itself a sensation, spontaneously carrying along with it belief in the existence of the object. This outcome was a direct result of the metaphysical standpoint already indicated:

the image as such loses its character of an immediate given. To become aware that a given object is now given *as imagined* calls for a certain procedure on my part.

This brings us to the second solution to the problem of "the characteristics of the true image." According to Taine, the proponent of this solution, there occurs a mechanical discrimination of sensations from images.

> The ordinary image thus is not a simple fact but a double one. It is a spontaneous and consistent sensation which undergoes diminution, limitation, and correction in conflict with another sensation which is neither spontaneous nor primitive. Two moments are involved: in the first, it seems external and localised, in the second, this externality and localisation are removed. The outcome of a struggle, an image has a tendency to appear external when attacked and overcome by the contrary and stronger tendency brought into play at the same time by the excited nerve.[7]

Thus the awareness of an image is mediated, and the battle between the two sensations is merely an episode in the Darwinian struggle for life, where the stronger carries the day. Taine was careful to add that victory may remain on the side of the "coherent and spontaneous" sensation, in which case hallucination occurs. In order for an image to be recognized as an image, that is, "to have its normal effect," there must be an *opposing* sensation. Failing this—or should the image happen to be stronger—we have before us an object which *in fact* does not exist.

Such a view is obscure indeed. Is it physiological or psychological? Where does the discriminating take place?

Taine appeared hesitant and unwilling to make the choice. Sometimes we are led to believe that sensations and images oppose each other as conscious events.

> As memory comes back, images and ideas reappear which sweep the image into their procession, engage it in battle, dominate it, snatch it from its solitary career, bring it back into a social existence, submerge it once more into its customary state of dependence.[8]

At other times we are given a description of a veritable mechanism of cortical inhibition.

> When a hallucinating person, eyes wide open, sees three feet from him a figure where there is only a wall papered in grey with green stripes, the figure covers and renders invisible a portion of the wall. Thus, the sensations which that portion of the wall should have stimulated were absent. Yet the retina and very likely the optical centers were excited in the usual way by the grey and green bands. In other words, the image which prevailed annihilated the portion of sensation which would have contradicted it.[9]

This certainly sounds like cortical inhibition, and one wonders why the sensations of gray and green are *inhibited* instead of simply being relegated to the rank of images. To tell the truth, Taine fails to decide because, as we saw above, he never had a clear conception of the difference between the physiological and the psychological.

Furthermore, how is this "correction," this "righting action," to be understood? The spontaneous coherent sensation is at first *located* and *external*. And Taine cites a whole host of examples. The bookseller Nicolai saw a figure of death "ten feet away." An English painter "gets" his models "from his mind" and "seats them on a chair." A friend of Darwin, having "looked very intently one day, head bent, at a small engraving of the Virgin and Child . . . was startled on looking up to see at the far end of the room the figure of a woman with a child in her arms." Then, under the influence of the opposing sensation, the spontaneous one loses location and externality. This is difficult to concede. Externality was not a relation but an intrinsic quality of the first representation no less than of the second. How then could the first sensation have lost its externality through contact with a contrary impression? To be sure it is hard to conceive, for example, a man and a table in the same place. But if the man is "ten feet away," the presence of a table at the same place will not stop him from being ten feet away. And perhaps Taine, whose vocabulary like his mind was not precise, confused externality and objectivity. But the difficulty remains unchanged. What mechanical opposition could render subjective an image that first declares itself an object?

What Taine needed is obvious. His associationism forbade him to fall back on a judgmental differentiation. But all his explanations pointed toward an associationist equivalent of a judgment made out of mechanical operations. In this he failed. First of all, his concept of a "contradictory sensation"[10] stealthily borrowed from judgment one of its qualities. Only two judgments, indeed, can contradict each other. I cannot assert of the same object at the same time, "It is white," and "It is not white." Two sensations cannot contradict each other, but mingle. If I do project "ten feet away" an image of a square of white cloth, and at the same distance and moment there is a square of black cloth, there will not be two opposed objects holding each other in check; rather, I will see a square of gray cloth. Thus to grant that sensations and images mutually exclude each other, the term "image" must already have been understood to mean a judgment.

A further comment will make the point still clearer. I am in my room, sitting at my desk. I hear the faint sounds made by the maid in the next apartment. At the same time I distinctly recall, in its rhythm, its timbre, its intonation, a statement I heard uttered the day before yesterday. How can the faint creaks in the next apartment "reduce" the "coherent sensation" of the statement when they cannot even drown out the faint sound of voices from the street below? Would we not have to say that the creaking sounds distinguished between what had to be cut out and what should be given passage? Would not such creaking sensations already be *judgmental?* Otherwise, if we are to credit Taine's theory with logical rigor, would I not *have* to have an auditory hallucination? If so, then I shall not have a hundred or a thousand hallucinations, but an endless series of them. For the silence of my room and of the countryside are not sensations and could not function as "reducing agents." Does deafness suffice for a veritable craze of connections?

Moreover, alongside the notion of a purely mechanical and doubtless physiological counteraction, that in spite of itself appeals to judgment, there is in Taine the suggestion of another theory that explicitly assigns a role to judgment. For it was Taine who wrote:

> Besides the weight provided by sensation, there are other weights which, though lighter, ordinarily suffice in a state of good health to strip the image of its

> externality. I refer to memories, which are themselves images, but coordinated and lying at a distance that locates them along a time scale. . . . General judgments gained in experience link up with them, and all together they form a group of interrelated elements, in equilibrium with each other, such that the whole acquires a great deal of cohesion and lends its strength to each of the elements.[11]

True enough, two pages later, fearful no doubt of the consequences of this explanation, which threatened to ruin the mechanistic theory of counteragents, Taine added:

> When an image reaching extraordinary intensity cancels out the particular sensation which is its specific counteragent, we have an hallucination, for all the memories that may occur and for all the judgments that may be instituted. Actually, we know we are hallucinating, but the image seems, nonetheless, external. Our other sensations and our other images continue to constitute a group in equilibrium, but this counteragent is not enough because it is not specific.[12]

In sum, Taine's theory of counteragents or "reducing" agents is an attempt to translate into mechanistic terms a more subtle and profound theory that entrusts to the spontaneity of judgment the task of distinguishing image and sensation. This latter conception—the only one to be reckoned with, implicit in the other two—must now be examined. We have already encountered it in Descartes, where we saw its defects within the Cartesian system. We now need to explain in wholly general terms why it is unsatisfactory.

The starting point is once again the assertion that

sensations and images are identical in nature. Once again we hear that an image *in isolation* is indistinguishable from a perception *in isolation*. This time, however, the distinction is to result from a judging act of the mind. Judgment is to constitute two worlds, the imaginary and the real, deciding when they are constituted whether such and such a psychic content should be allocated to the one or the other. The only question remaining concerns the *characteristics* according to which a judgment is to be made. The answer can only be in terms of external relations, that is to say, on the one hand, the mode of appearing, of succession, and of linkage, and on the other hand, the compatibility or incompatibility of the contemplated content with the worlds we have constituted. Whatever would not be compatible with the coherence and order of the real world, which we have learned during long apprenticeship to recognize and construct, we relegate to the subjective side. Defending this thesis, Spaier wrote:

> **By judging the agreement or disagreement of a sensuous atom with either the system of my actual external world or with that of my imagination (distinguishable from the former through long and endless tests), by passing judgments of comparison, adequacy, inadequacy, membership, etc., I classify an impression among real perceptions or among images.**[13]

Two comments are in order. First, the criterion of truth has undergone an evolution. No longer concerned with a relation of conformity to an external object, we are in a world of representations. The criterion has become the agreement of representations with each other.

We are thus freed from a naive realism. But the index of truth remains external to the representation itself, for comparison determines whether or not it should be incorporated into the grouping of "reality." Second, the problem of "the characteristics of a true image" has radically changed its meaning. No longer are there "image" data or "object" data. Rather, on the basis of neutral data an objective system is to be constructed. The real world is not; rather, it is made, receiving constant retouching, elaboration, and enrichment. Such and such a grouping, long held to be objective, is finally rejected; such and such another grouping, long isolated, is suddenly incorporated in the system. The problem of distinguishing images is one with that of constructing objectivity. An image is that among sensuous data which cannot succeed to objectivity. An image is subjectivity itself. Never have we strayed so far from the province of the psychological: instead of the nature of the image as such being revealed to us in an immediate intuition,[14] we must ultimately introduce an infinite system of references to be able to declare a content image or perception. In practice, of course, we are satisfied with a few well-chosen comparisons. But there follows the rather serious consequence that the differentiating judgment will never be anything but probable. Thus Maldidier spoke in the article cited earlier of "the *probable* characteristics of the true image." Indeed, only a comparative investigation carried to infinite lengths could yield certainty, and the reference system is constantly changing itself. For example, an atheistic positivist would accept dogmas and believe in miracles following a conversion and would no longer have the same reference system as before. We are thus led to the paradoxical conclusion that far from the fundamental nature of the image being revealed to us through an immediate and certain apprehension [*connaissance*], we would never be sure such and such a psychic content which appeared at such and such a moment was indeed an image. Introspection would be entirely divested of its rights in favor of judgment, and consciousness confronting its own data would assume the hypothetical, experimental attitude normally adopted in the face of the external world.

The artificial nature of this account is only too obvious. No one would grant that to establish the difference between an image and a perception one must resort to an infinite reference system. Let everyone consult his own inner experience. I am seated, writing, and see the things around me. Suddenly I form an image of my friend Peter. All the theories in the world are helpless against the fact that I *knew,* the very instant of the appearance of the image, that it was an image. The example Spaier cited to support his theory [15] proved nothing. He wrote of a faint pattering that he heard one day before going out.

> **Was it starting to rain? I listened, I listened again. I found that the noise persisted. There was a first observation, an initial *sign.* Was I then satisfied? Not at all. *For,* my ears might be ringing. I went to the window. No water on the pane. But rain may fall straight down. *Consequently,* I opened the window and leaned out . . . etc.[16]**

Who ever went to such lengths to distinguish an image from a perception? If the image of a noise had crossed my awareness, I would have recognized it on the spot as an image without having to look at the glass or open the window. To be sure, let us grant that the scene reported by Spaier was not simply invented for the occasion. But a serious error crept into his reasoning. This series of tests (taking up two pages of descriptions) was not undertaken to distinguish the image of a noise from a perception, but a false perception from a true one. Naturally, if the only difference allowed between an image and a perception is the difference between the false and the true, every image is fated to be termed a false perception. This is precisely what no psychologist can admit. To perceive a man where a tree stands is not to form an image of a man, but merely to perceive a tree poorly. One remains on the terrain of perception, and up to a point one perceives rightly: there is indeed an object in the shadows, ten feet away. It is indeed a thin body, slender, about six feet tall, etc. But the deception lay in the manner of grasping the *import* or *meaning* of the object. Similarly, if I cock my ear to ascertain whether I did indeed hear a pitter-patter, this means at bottom that I am trying to determine whether what I heard *was indeed a pitter-patter*. I may have taken an organic sound, the sound of my breathing, for example, for a patter of rain.[17]

Moreover, facing the issue on the very terrain chosen by Spaier, how can one say that a judgment, by classing a representation among images, manages at the same time to cancel its externality? Taine, who had a notion of a discrimination effected by judgment, was under no illusion. He wrote, as we saw:

> **The range of memories may well subsist, and judgments may well be made, yet one has a hallucination. One realizes that one is hallucinating, but the image appears no less external.**

This is just what seems required by Spaier's hypothesis. If I see a man sitting across from me, a judgment may well convince me it is a vision, a phantom. For all that, I do not cease to see the man sitting across from me. Or are we to believe that judgment carves out and erects externality and internality parallel to each other within a group of neutral psychic contents? This is contrary to common sense and to the actual data of the problem of perception.

But even if it were admitted that this differentiating process might occasionally succeed, it would not function in the majority of cases. First one would often have to take perceptions for images. A host of strange little occurrences take place about us at every moment, objects which apparently move of their own accord, cracking or groaning, appearing or disappearing, and the like. On reflection all these fantastic occurrences are readily explicable, but initially they should startle us. We should be tempted, at least for a second, to class them as images. I was sure that I put my hat in the closet, and there it is on the chair. Do I fall into doubt, "disbelieving my eyes"? Not for a second. I might wear myself out looking for explanations, but I would take for granted in all my reflections from start to finish, without even bothering to go over and touch the felt, that the hat I see is *my real hat*. I think my friend Peter is in America. There he is at the corner of the street. Do I say, "It's an image"? Not at all. My first reaction is to wonder how he could possibly be back already. Was he called back? Is someone ill in his family? In fact, I remember one day running into an old school friend whom I believed to be dead. Actually, two memories had contaminated each other, but I would have sworn that I had received word of his death. This belief did not keep my first thought, the moment I saw him, from being: "I was wrong. It wasn't he who died, it must have been so and so, etc." What does all this indicate? That far from rational factors being capable of casting doubt on our perceptions, our perceptions rule and guide our judgments and reasoning. To them we constantly adapt our frames of reference. I may be convinced that X is dead or on a long trip. If I see him, I *revise* my judgments. Perception is a prime source of knowledge, proffering us the objects themselves. It is what the Germans call an "original giving intuition" (*originär gebende Anschauung*),[18] and we realize this so keenly that our mental attitude toward perception runs contrary to Spaier's account. Far from criticizing it, once it takes place, we seek only to justify it in every way. Some people, believing that they have seen Peter, even though Peter could not possibly be in France (since he was seen boarding the ship for New York three days ago), will maintain the rights of their false perception against the rights of reason by the most sophistical and implausible arguments. What is more, most of the time this method of differentiation would be quite inadequate for detecting images. Its success would depend on our imaginings being for the most part fantastic, unreasonable, lyrical, and so different from our everyday perceptions that judgment could expel them with some probability from the real world. Instead, what is, in the main, the imaginary world in which I live? Well, I am waiting for my friend Peter, who could arrive at any moment, and I form a representation of his face. Last night I went to John's house, and I recall what he was wearing. I then think of the detachable collars in my dresser, then of my inkwell, etc. etc. Nothing real contradicts all these familiar images. The door opens onto darkness. Nothing prevents me from projecting an image of Peter on that black background. Were I to do so, I would have no reason at all to doubt the reality of the image, since he has a latchkey. But, it will be asked, what if he does not advance toward you? What if he does not reply when you speak? What if he disappears all of a sudden? Unquestionably, I would then take him to be an hallucination. But who, I ask, who would dare say in all conscience that he ever resorted to such methods to classify an appearance as an image or as a perception? In fact, our train of images takes its cue most of the time from our train of perceptions, what we imagine merely preceding by a little bit what is coming up, or succeeding by a bit what has already occurred. On the theory discussed, perception thus would have to be at every moment a victory over dreams. On the merest supposition one would continually have to risk denying the reality of such and such a figure and affirming, without any cogent reason, the existence of such and such another figure. The world of sense, so laboriously constructed, would be perpetually invaded by the most likely looking images which one would nevertheless have to head off, for better or for worse, without ever being absolutely sure of being entitled to do so. Such a world, where one never stops connecting appearances, where every perception is a judgment and a victory, bears not the slightest resemblance to the world around us. Objects are relatively stable, relatively clear. No doubt one must often wait before being sure of the nature of an object, and this wait may well be considered the very essence of the perceptual outlook. Appearances which thus dissipate are not images, but merely incomplete aspects of things. No image ever mixes in with real things. This is fortunate indeed, for otherwise, as we have seen, we would have no way of heading them off, and the waking world would not be sharply distinguished from the dream world.

Thus, once a fundamental identity of perceptions and images has been asserted, one is forced to resort to probability judgments to distinguish them. But these probability judgments would never be able to find firm ground. The order of perceptions and the order of images would have to differentiate themselves from each other decisively and make possible a discrimination through judgment. Which amounts to saying that if the differentiation is not first *given* in some way, no power of understanding will suffice to bring it about. This could have been foreseen from the beginning. Start by asserting the essential identity of two things, and you have removed, by the very nature of such an affirmation, all possibility of distinguishing them later. The metaphysical theory of images thus fails conclusively in the attempt to arrive at the spontaneous awareness of an image, and the first step of a concrete psychology must be to get rid of metaphysical postulates. The starting point, instead, is the following unimpeachable given: I cannot possibly form an image without at the same time knowing that I am forming an image; and the immediate knowledge I have of the image as such may become the basis for judgments of existence (of the type of "I have an image of X," "This is an image," etc.), but it is itself *prepredicative* evidence.

No doubt we could find more than one psychologist

today who would grant us this principle, but few see clearly what their acknowledgment commits them to. Thus, in the article cited above, Meyerson could write:

> **An image is not a weakened perception or sensation. It is not a pale reflection of the past. An image is on the road to abstraction and generalization, on the road to thought. An image is thus a perception thought over [*repensée*] and, however weathered it may nevertheless appear, rationalized. It is already a reasoned form of the sensory given.[19]**

To declare that an image is not a perception is well and good. But a declaration is not enough. The assertion must be buttressed by consistent description of the psychic fact known as an "image." If one ends up implicitly confounding image and perception, there is no point in crying so loudly that they are indeed distinguished. What is more, one need only read the passage just quoted with a little attention to see that Meyerson's description of images would fit perceptions word for word. An image, it is said, is a "rationalization of the sensory given." But is it otherwise in perception? Are there perceptions which are not acts of thought? Are there perceptions which are pure sensory givens, without any intentional synthesis? An image is "on the road to abstraction, to generalization." Does this mean that there are no absolutely individual images? In the first place, this is not quite so, but is an erroneous interpretation of a real fact which we shall try to explain elsewhere.[20] But even if it were so, would it not be exactly as true of perception as well? I am perceiving "an inkwell," "a table," "a Louis XVI armchair." To attain the individual, the sensory stuff, *this particular hue* of the upholstery of the chair,

I must make an effort, reversing the direction of attention.[21] Or, as Spaier has said, someone smiles and I perceive good will, someone waves a flag and I perceive the nation, the party or class emblem. Am I not then more than halfway on the road to abstraction and generalization? If I compare the perception of *a* house (I saw a flag in the window of *a* house) to the memory-image of *the* house in which I spent my childhood, which of these two acts of consciousness is on the side of generality, which on the side of particularity? An image is a perception thought over, wrote Meyerson. When is it rethought? Are we to fancy the propitious shadows of an unconscious where, unperceived, a nice little job of polishing up could be done? Or shall we say that the transformation occurs the moment the image comes to consciousness? But in this case why *re*think this reviving perception? Why didn't we *think* it when it appeared the first time? Like many contemporary psychologists, Meyerson did draw the required distinction, but without knowing why.

The passages just quoted show us clearly what is entailed in the assertion that "there is a difference in kind between perceptions and images." Meyerson in some sense distinguished matter and form in images. The matter is the sensory given.[22] This is likewise the matter of perception. But the form received is different, that is, the image is pervaded by reason. The failure of his attempt at a distinction, however, demonstrates that form will not suffice to distinguish images from perceptions. Doubtless we shall see later that the *intention* [23] proper to an image is not that of a perception. But we must add that images and perceptions do not have the same matter either. We encounter here the famous Aristotelian problem of whether it is form or matter that individualizes. Our answer, so far as images are concerned, is: both. If, as one would think, the matter of perception is the sensory given, then the matter of the image cannot be sensory. If the psychic structure called an "image" has in any manner a reviving sensation at its base—even a rationalized and rearranged one—it becomes utterly impossible by any procedure whatsoever to establish any distinction at all between image and reality, between the waking world and the world of dreams.

B. The relations between images and thoughts

Images are thus almost universally regarded as having a sensory content, that is to say, an impressional matter identical with that of perception. This matter calls for a measure of receptivity in the mind, for it is something irrational, a *given*. If one admits, as Spaier does, that "to become conscious [*prendre conscience*] [24] is to take note," then there must be something at the base of the image which simply *is* and allows itself to be noted. And this is the case, it will be added, in perception. No doubt. But of course the perceived object stands over against our thoughts, imposing itself on them. We are forced to fashion the sequence of our ideas by reference to the perceived object, *waiting on it,* making hypotheses about its character, observing it. Is this attitude possible —meaningful even—with regard to an image, with regard to something which appears as an aid to thought? An image enables one to decipher, to understand, to explain. Must it, too, first be deciphered, understood, explained? How so? By means of another image? To tell the truth, these difficulties that stand out so plainly were inevitable, since an image, although assimilated at the outset to perception, is surely thought. We *form* images, we *construct* schemata.[25] The majority of authors inevitably complicate matters by making the image an external object and then, to boot, an idea. Thus, after having shown that to distinguish an image from a perception one must resort to judgment and even to reasoning, Spaier did not balk at writing as follows:

> There are not images on the one hand, and ideas on the other. There are only more or less concrete concepts.

True enough, after having tried to throw light on the way in which images are elaborated and schematized by thought he emphasized concomitantly the part played in external perception by constructs. Images are always significant—for perceptions are always judgments.

> Raw sensations no more exist than do pure images, and thus neither can prevent us from identifying consciousness, together with the most sensory of its contents, and thinking.

Yet the fact that sensory contents are rationalized by thought obviously does not mean that they are *identical* with thought. Quite the contrary. Moreover, beneath these solid-looking statements one detects a drifting of ideas. For Spaier an image does not have the same *function* as a perception, displaying rather a mobility, a transparency, and a docility by which it can be assimilated to judgmental, discursive thought. But if *this* is how images are thoughts, then a perception is not a thought, and sensory content constitutes the externality and objectivity of perception. How can we say that *here* the sensory content opposes consciousness and calls for observation, waiting, and conjecture, and *there* it participates in the fluidity, mobility, and transparency of the subjective? In a word, if an image has a sensory content, perhaps one could think *on* it, but never *with* it.

Such participation of images in the sensory might be conceived in two ways, following Descartes or following Hume.

Descartes' theory of imagination, as we have seen, is located at the psychophysiological level. There is a mind *and* there is a body. An image is an idea formed by the soul on the occasion of a modification of the body. Setting aside Cartesian terminology, we may say that psychosensory centers may be excited by an internal or an external stimulus. An "image" corresponds to the former type of stimulation, a "perception" corresponds to the latter type. The basis of this contention is the assertion that nerve cells or groups of nerve cells can return, under various influences, to the condition which an external stimulus had brought about—a possibility which may be called a brain trace or an engram. But if this were so, the order of appearance of images in consciousness would result from the career of the "animal spirits," depending upon associative circuits and the path of the neural inflow. In a word, the succession of images in consciousness would be governed by a physiological determinism. This or that representation would surge into consciousness when this or that associative group is "reawakened." How, then, could an image be an effective aid to thought?

Descartes anticipated this objection, and supposed a sort of physiological contingency which would allow the soul to guide the animal spirits at will. We saw earlier that this strange theory is unacceptable. There remains the hypothesis of a thoroughgoing physiological determinism. The order of appearance of images, as Claparède clearly saw, would be governed by the real, material contiguity of brain "traces" in space.[26] The succession of images would thereby be governed by mechanical, objective laws. The image would become a part of the external world. No doubt it would be first and foremost a psychological act, but an act corresponding strictly to a physiological modification. Otherwise stated, we would have to *wait for* our images as we wait for objects, and hope for the image of Peter as I hope for the arrival in person of my friend Peter. What about thought, then? It would stand face to face with images, just as it stands face to face with perceptions, and would be what is not image and what is not perception. The trouble is that thought could not summon up images for assistance, any more than it could call forth an external object. These premises granted, one would also have to accept the comments made by William James (cited, incidentally, by Claparède in his work). On the occasion of a perception, the thought of something similar could not bring forth an image resembling the perception. Rather, the mechanics of contiguity would bring forth the image at the same time as the perception or image being inspected, and only then would thought be able to note the similarity. Thought, in short, could not function as the guiding theme around which images would organize themselves, as utensils, as approximations. Thought would be definitively reduced to the sole function of grasping relationships between two sorts of objects, thing-objects and image-objects. As Alain said, with a scarcely different meaning in mind: "We do not think as we wish." All well and good. But now what happens to the laws of logic? Doubtless one might try to reduce these, too, to associational connections, thus returning in one form or another to Taine's associationism. However, if we are to maintain the autonomy of thought, we will now be forced to reduce thought to the one immediate judgment which affirms at a given moment such and such a relation between two perceptions, two images, or an image and a perception, appearing outside and seemingly in despite of thought. In such thought, bumping along and splintering, transfixed in all its processes by ever fresh appearances without logical interrelations, who would recognize the faculty of reasoning, conceiving, devising machines, undertaking mental experiments, etc.?

There is only one way out: to accept a thoroughgoing parallelism of the modes of extension and thought. There would be bodily modifications corresponding to logical thought as well, and there would be no reason why these new modifications should not induce by a purely physiological mechanism the "reawakening" of traces corresponding to images. In this way one could allow for thought, which chooses its images and to a certain extent modifies their order of appearance. At least, *viewed from the mechanistic standpoint,* there would be no impossibility here. But no one will fail to realize that a thoroughgoing parallelism is admissible only in a Spinozistic metaphysics. If he had had to conceive bodily mechanisms as directing and explaining the succession of psychic facts, the spontaneity of consciousness would have vanished and the laws of logical thought would have been reduced to mere symbols of physiological laws. The net result would then be epiphenomenalism. Consequently we should have to conceive this parallelism quite otherwise; that is, as Spinoza never tired of repeating, a thought would have to be explained by another thought, and a motion by another motion. So that this parallelism, by trying to explain everything, explains nothing, at least, nothing of the psychological. It comes down to the declaration that the domain of consciousness must be studied in terms of consciousness and the domain of the physiological in physiological terms. Wishing to find a mechanical system which would account for the organizing power of thought, we find ourselves referred back to consciousness and forced to formulate the question in strictly psychological terms. We cannot maintain Cartesian dualism, and must give up explanations by traces, neural contiguity, etc. We may grant if we wish that some bodily modification corresponds to every image and every thought, but precisely for that reason the body explains nothing, and we are forced to envisage the relationship between thoughts and images as it appears to consciousness.

Thus we are necessarily led to consider the image's participation in the sensory from the second point of view,[27] that of Hume. At the outset, Hume knew nothing of the body, and began—or thought he began—with the immediate data of experience. There are strong impressions and faint impressions, the latter being images and differing from the former in intensity only. By this shift in viewpoint, have we overcome the difficulties encountered earlier? We think not. We propose to show that the difficulties do not turn on the point of view selected, but on the conception of an image as a sensory content.

The primary characteristic of impressions, for Hume, is in fact their "opaqueness." This very opacity it is that constitutes their character as sensory. Nor could anything be truer, so far as perceptions go. There is in the end something irreducible, incomprehensible, *given* about the yellow color of this ashtray, the roughness of that piece of wood. This given shows not only the opacity of perception, but also its receptivity, these being indeed only two sides of the same reality. Hume did not limit himself, however, to describing the sensory contents of perception. He wanted to put together the world of consciousness by means of these contents alone, which is to say, he doubled the perceptual order with an order of images which are the same sensory contents at a lower degree of intensity. The images of associationism thus represent centers of opaqueness and receptivity. Reborn in the guise of a weakened impression, the yellow color of this ashtray retains its character of *givenness*. It remains something irreducible, something irrational. Above all, and precisely because it is sheer passivity, it remains an *inert* element. What does this mean? It means that an image could not bear within itself, in the intimacy of its own being, the reason for its appearance. Of its own accord, it could neither revive nor disappear. It has to be evoked or rejected by something other than itself. This "something else," however, could not be a systematizing spontaneity, for a spontaneity could never contain portions of passivity. Either spontaneity is activity through and through, and consequently transparent to itself, or there is no such thing. The positing of sensory contents transports us into a world of pure externality, a world whose inert contents are determined in their modes of appearing by other, equally inert contents, a world in which all changes and all impulsions come from the outside and remain radically external to the content they set into motion. This is why the basic laws of associationism necessarily contained a sort of implicit assertion of the principle of inertia. They did not miss the mark. What after all is the law of resemblance if not a positing of external relations between psychic contents? It is after all accidental that Peter resembles John. What, above all, is the law of contiguity, if not a pure and simple translation of the principle of inertia into psychological terms? According to this law, the only connecting principle between two contents is encounter, contact. Thus, every content of consciousness is, in some sort, outside itself, for an impact makes it appear, an impact expels it from consciousness. We now see what consciousness really is for associationism: simply the world of things. Only a world of externality exists, the external world. There is no difference between this red ball and the perception of it. The ball is an inert body that remains still so long as no force arrives to set it in motion, but continues its motion into infinity if nothing impedes it. The perception of this ball is an inert content which could not appear without being shoved to the center of consciousness by some other content, but which would remain present indefinitely, once it had appeared, if nothing were to push it out. Laporte was right in comparing Hume to the Neo-Realists. For him, as for them, there are only objects, in external relations, and consciousness is nothing but a collection of these objects viewed from the standpoint of a certain kind of relation (the laws of association). But then what is the difference, it may be asked, between the law of contiguity as understood by Descartes and as given by associationism? The answer is: none. The Cartesian law of contiguity has to do with brain traces, is understood in a spatial sense, and rests explicitly on the principle of inertia. The associationist law of contiguity is also derived from the principle of inertia, and likewise implies externality and contact, even if not in a strictly spatial sense. Only, for Descartes associative connections are made between the imprints left by the objects, whereas for Hume they link up the objects themselves.

Hume was perfectly consistent, however, and his system must be accepted or rejected as a whole. Having assumed that the elements of consciousness are passive in their nature, he applied the principle of inertia to the psychic domain and reduced consciousness to a collection of inert contents linked by external relations. One would think, therefore, that any allegedly "synthetic" psychology claiming a spontaneity at the heart of consciousness would have to renounce unequivocally all the theses of Hume. Naturally, one would have to grant the existence of sensory contents in perception. By this very fact, however, one would recognize that the order in which they succeed each other is strictly independent of consciousness. The appearance of sensory contents would thus remain under the governance of a certain sort of association. Husserl's way of expressing this was to say that the principle of the relation between sensory contents is *passive genesis by association,* whose essential form is temporal flow.[28] Psychological consciousness[29] could never control the succession, but as act every consciousness "takes heed of it" [*la "constate"*], in Spaier's phrase. With this heeding, whose structures constitute a special subject matter for description, perception of the external world takes place.

On turning to images, however, one would expect a psychology of synthesis to deny firmly any sensory origin and any assimilation to "faint impressions." A choice must be made: either images remain inert contents, in which case the role of spontaneity must be limited to the apperception of relations between images which elicit each other according to the laws of association; or, consciousness is organization, systematization, and the flow of psychic facts is guided by controlling themes, in which case the image can no longer be assimilated to an opaque, received content. Thus, nothing was gained by shifting to the level of pure psychology. On the contrary, the need to make a choice is more strongly felt, for there are no more psychophysiological escape-hatches.

The synthesis psychologists never made a choice. To be sure, they said that every state of mind is a synthesis, that the whole gives meaning to the parts, and that thought guides and selects its images. But they kept a sensory base for their images, and this was enough to falsify radically their psychology. Sensory contents, once posited, must be interrelated, in one way or another, by laws of association, which are the only laws appropriate to the inert. Consequently very few psychologists will categorically deny the laws of association. So much do these laws seem to *belong* to the sensory given that they are retained on some lower level, in dreams, distraction, "low tension" areas. At the very same time a continual harmony between images actually present in consciousness and directive themes, actually governing thought, is acknowledged. How is this possible? Thought *chooses* its images, we are told. But how is choosing to occur? Are the laws of association suspended, or does thought turn them to its own account? The whole problem posed by Cartesian physiology thus reappears on the level of pure psychology. A while ago we were wondering how thought could direct the animal spirits and turn contiguities in the brain to its own account. Now we may raise the same question in scarcely different terms. How can thought direct associations and turn psychological contiguity to its own account? There is of course no question of thought creating its images. How indeed could this spontaneity generate that which is opaque? So thought must hunt for them. Naturally, a storehouse of contents is invented for the occasion, known as the unconscious. We saw, indeed, how much Hume was handicapped by not having such a notion. He never actually invented it, but his whole psychology implied it. Modern writers appeal to it constantly. Yet is it not clear that this unconscious, where inert contents exist like things, neither *aware of* themselves nor existing *for* anyone, and where opaque data are related only by contact or by resemblance, is a spatial setting strictly assimilable to the brain?

Only the words have changed. If we are told that thought goes in search of images, thought is necessarily transformed into a physical force. An analogy promotes the confusion. In the external world are inert objects which I can take hold of, move about, remove from a drawer or put back. We seem to be able to conceive an *activity* which operates on passive givens. But the mistake is easily detected. If I can pick up this book or that cup, it is in so far as I am an organism, a body also subject to the laws of inertia. The mere fact that I can oppose my thumb to my four fingers in a clutching gesture already presupposes the whole of mechanics. Here is only the appearance of activity. Hence it is impossible to assign to thought an evoking power over inert contents without at once materializing thought. To turn a positive power to evoke into a negative power of selection only appears to resolve the difficulty. To set aside presupposes physical grasping power, action through contact, no less than evoking does. I am misled by a figure of speech, I shall be told. When thought is said to evoke, to set aside, to select, the speech is figurative. No doubt that is so. But we should like to know what underlies these figures of speech. If the terms are metaphorical, let us know the reality hiding behind the words. Obviously, however, there is nothing beneath the words, behind the figures of speech, because there can be nothing there. That exists spontaneously which determines its own existence. In other words, to exist spontaneously is to exist for oneself and through oneself [*exister pour soi et par soi*]. One reality alone deserves to be called "spontaneous": consciousness. To exist and to be conscious of existing are one and the same for consciousness. Otherwise stated, the supreme ontological law of consciousness is as follows: for a consciousness the only way of existing is to be conscious that it exists. It is therefore evident that consciousness can determine itself to exist, but that it cannot act on anything but itself. A sensory content may be the occasion for our forming a consciousness, but we cannot act by means of consciousness on the sensory content, dragging it from nowhere (or from the unconscious), or sending it back. If images are consciousness, they are pure spontaneities. Consciousness of itself, self-transparency, and existing only to the extent that it knows itself, an image therefore cannot be a sensory content. It is perfectly futile to represent it as "rationalized," as "permeated by thought." There is no middle ground: either it is wholly thought, and one thinks *by means of* the image, or it is sensory content and one would think *on the occasion of* an image. In the latter case, the image will be independent of consciousness, *appearing* to consciousness according to laws peculiar to an image which is not consciousness. Such an image, which must be awaited, deciphered, and observed, is simply a *thing*. Any inert and opaque content takes its place, by the necessity inherent in its type of existence, among objects, that is to say, in the external world. That there are only two types of existence, as thing in the world and as consciousness, is an ontological law.

A clear demonstration that images, once become "sensory contents," are expelled from thought, is that contemporary psychologists proceed to accept implicitly a radical distinction between the image and the thought of it. Hoernlé, we saw, distinguished the image and its meaning, that is, in effect, the image as a *thing* and what the image is *for thought*. Likewise [30] Spaier: "Our attention does not fall on the object of sensory intuition (the image or perception) but on the meaning." Here we have the image posited as an independent object apprehended in one way or another by thought, but existing *in itself* in a different way than it exists for consciousness. Spaier introduces an example valid beyond question —for perception: I *see* a smile (the edges of the lips are raised, the nostrils dilate, the eyebrows go up, etc.), and I *perceive* cordiality. But what does this mean? External to me there is a certain *thing*, a face, with its own existence. It is what it is, and has an infinite multitude of aspects. Also, it contains an infinity of details that I cannot see (pores, cells). Knowing this face involves an infinite approximation; hence it is infinitely richer than it appears, and I must wait, observe, make mistakes. Since the passage cited above explicitly assimilates images to perceptions, we are entitled to apply word for word to an image of a smiling face the foregoing description. The countenance reborn in an image must also have its pores, its cells, its multiplicity of aspects. Such being the definition of the transcendence of things, the image too is a thing, but we apprehend it in terms of its meaning. If we wish to escape from this tangle of difficulties and posit the image as a fact of consciousness, we shall have to give up any distinction between what it is and what it appears to be; or, if you like, we shall have to say that the mode of being of an image is precisely its "appearance" [*son "paraître"*].

We may conclude that any theory of imagination must satisfy two requirements. It must account for the spontaneous discrimination made by the mind between its images and its perceptions. And it must explain the role that images play in the operations of thought. Whatever form it took, the classical conception of images was unable to fulfill these two essential functions. To endow an image with a sensory content is to make it a thing obeying the laws of things, not the laws of consciousness. The mind is thus deprived of all hope of distinguishing images from the other things belonging in the world. By the same token, there is no way at all to conceive the relation of this thing to thought. Indeed, by removing images from consciousness, we deprive the latter of all its freedom, and by introducing images into consciousness, the whole universe follows after, solidifying consciousness at one stroke, like a supersaturated solution.

Understandable indeed, the ensuing offensive mapped out, before the [first world] war, against the image. It is an obstacle to thought, Binet and several Würzburg psychologists were saying. Others went further, remarking that if an image must be grounded in revived sensory contents we are then forced to accept associationism, atomistic psychology, and the juxtaposition of contents of thought. So an image must rather be a mere entity of reason that was allowable only during the time in which the theory of cerebral localization held sway. Confronted by the hypotheses of Broca and Wernicke, it vanishes, quite out of place in a synthetic psychology. Moutier, a follower of Marie, wrote in 1908:

> The great mistake concerning images was to believe in them as realities. Their purely hypothetical and conventional reality was lost sight of, and bit by bit they became detached from words and ideas. Finally, the brain was conceded to have images without words, without ideas, without a single attribute, in short, pure images. Images of words were contrasted to words as such, and ideas were disengaged from words and from images. The culmination was the discovery that inner speech may exist in three ways, by means of words, through images of words, and by means of pure ideas. What is true of "thinking substance" is true of images. They are metaphysical "realities" corresponding to nothing ever experienced.[31]

This viewpoint, which expressed the spirit of synthesis in purest form, refused to countenance elements isolated in psychic life. But it was rather unclear. For one thing, it moved on the dubious level of physiological psychology. Images and ideas are described as being "in the brain." Just what this means, we do not know. Is this a physiological hypothesis according to which the brain functions like the heart or the liver, an organ in the unity of a biological synthesis? Is it a psychological theory of the indivisibility of a psychic state? Or is it both at once? And to what extent is the reality of images denied? Should we perhaps think of the image as a "metaphysical reality," an "abstraction," as the individual is for some sociologists? In this case, we need only understand that an image has no reality *functionally* speaking, that it is never independent. But this leads us right back to Spaier's view. Or should we see here a radical denial of the image as a structure of consciousness? Or is it rather the trace-image of Broca that Moutier wished to reject? To tell the truth, Moutier was no psychologist. He was defending the unity of the living creature against the analytical tendencies of a Broca or a Taine. That was progress, no doubt, but only in method. Moutier had no more concern for the direct testimony of consciousness than Taine did. He *deduced* his denial of images from general, abstract principles. Taine had selected the image as a unique explanatory principle because he was trying to construct a scientific psychology on the model of physics. Similarly, because the emerging biology had introduced the notion of organic synthesis, and because he saw, more perspicacious than Ribot, that the notion of synthesis is incompatible with the notion of psychic atoms, Moutier assigned images to "metaphysical entities," without any more inspection of the concrete data than Taine had undertaken. The procedure was the same in both cases.[32]

C. The theory of Alain

A theory of knowledge and of judgment were responsible for the radical denial of images voiced by Alain.

> That we keep copies of things in our memory, that we can in some sense riffle through them, is a simple and convenient enough notion, but a little too puerile.[33]

Images do not exist, could not exist. What we call by this name is always a false perception.

> In every fact of imagination, three sorts of causes are present: the external world, the bodily state, and motions.[34]

Every false perception, however, is merely a false judgment, since perceiving is judging. A mob in Metz thought they saw an army in the windowpanes of a building. They *thought* they saw it, but they did not see it. There were lines, colors, reflections, but no army. Nor was there a "representation" of an army in their minds. There was no *projection* of an image onto the glass, no memory was blended with the data of perception. Fear and haste led to a hurried judgment, a misinterpretation.

> When we imagine that we can hear a voice in the ticking of a clock, we never hear anything but a clock ticking, and the least bit of attention to the matter tells us so. But in such a case, and doubtless in every case, the false judgment is sustained by the voice itself, and the voice creates a new object replacing the other. We forge the imagined thing, and by that very token it is real, and beyond doubt is perceived . . .[35] A strong emotion is felt and per-

ceived, inseparable from bodily movements and at the same time a belief occurs which is plausible enough, but anticipatory and ultimately lacking an object. The whole thing has the character of an impassioned expectation, imaginary in one sense but real enough through the tumult of the body. . . . Disorder in the body, error in the mind, the one nurturing the other, such is the reality of imagination.

Our earlier exposition enables us to understand, we would contend, the position of this Cartesian rationalist. Like Descartes, Alain accepted as an initial postulate a fundamental identity of images and perceptions. A more profound and more circumspect thinker than the psychologists we have undertaken to criticize, however, he was immediately struck by the ensuing contradictions. It is absurd to suppose that there can be images exactly similar to perceptions and to go on to suppose that one could distinguish between them. However, having accepted that products of imagination may be distinguished from objects of perception as error from truth, might we not save the day by reversing the account? To distinguish images from perceptions by the external criteria of the true and the false is necessarily to declare that *all false perceptions are images*. Such, we have seen, was the method of Spaier. But then the famous "revived sensory content" is left over and inexplicable. Why not rather say, beginning with the same principles, that *all images are false perceptions?* In that case, the "reviving sensation" is no longer called for. The only sensory data are those presently furnished by my perception. Depending on whether I judge truly or falsely, I constitute these data as real objects or as phantoms. These phantoms are images. Naturally, there are several kinds of imagination. One type, externally oriented, consists of false judgments of external objects. The other, inwardly aimed, "turns away from things, eyes closed, heeding in particular the movements of life and the faint impressions which they induce." The real object that judgment may falsify by too great haste and emotion is the coenesthetic given—or even a thousand fleeting perceptions, after-images, entoptic spots. Thus, there would never be independent representations with their own content and an autonomous life, for an image is but a falsified perception. As a result we would no longer need to ask about the way in which images "link" together. Without revived sensory contents, there can be no association of ideas, and no selection made by thought. One judges present sensory contents, which succeed each other as required by the laws of the world. "Our dreams come from the world, not from the gods." Thought would be spontaneous judgment—true, or false—of the present data of the external world and of the body. Here we meet once more that notion, to which we called attention earlier, that restricts thought to judgment. Before, however, this judgmental thinking was hindered and joggled by the dual sequence of "sensory" images and perceptions. Alain freed thought from the order of images. Thought takes its cue from the world, before which it stands alone.

> **We do not think as we please. We think that we think as we please because the ideas which come to a man's mind are almost always suitable to the circumstances. If I stroll along the docks, the sequence of my ideas does not differ much from the sequence of things I see—cranes, mounds of coal, boats, carts, barrels. If I do pursue some daydream once in a**

> while, it does not stay longer than a bird on the wing. Some live impression soon thrusts me back among the things surrounding me; and as I watch out for myself among these masses that ascend, descend, turn, grind, and knock into each other, my attention is thereby disciplined and I establish in my mind true relations between real things.
>
> But where do they come from, these flights of reverie that cut across my perceptions from time to time? If I were to look carefully I would almost always find some real object glimpsed only for a moment—a bird in the sky, a tree in the distance, or a man's face turned toward me for a second and spilling out at my feet, in a flash, a rich cargo of hopes, fears, angers. Our thoughts are copied after things which are present, and our capacity for dreaming is not so extensive as is claimed.
>
> I remember discussing these matters with a friend. We were strolling at random in the woods. He was asking if we are not able to draw treasures out of ourselves, as from a coffer, without the assistance of something present to us. At the very moment the word "Byrrh" [36] came to mind, which certainly had no relation to the trees and birds. I told him. We talked about it. We came to a sort of shack half-swallowed by branches. As I glanced at it, I saw a poster nailed on the window—on which was inscribed the word "Byrrh." [37]

Alain's theory was especially devised to avoid the contradictions noted in the present chapter. One must acknowledge that it succeeds in its aim, but only by giving up the very notion of an image. A more appropriate conclusion to our critical exposition could not be found: if mental images are assimilated to perceptions, the image destroys itself, and one is led, like Alain, to a theory of imagination without any images.

Can we possibly accept this? We think not. Conceived a priori, like the others, it is a theory that does not square with the facts. By not consulting the testimony of consciousness Alain eliminated images, and thereby attributed to imagination both too much and too little.

Too much, for he necessarily viewed imagination as belief in a false object. I stroll along a dark road at night. I take fright. My fear hurries my power of judgment and I take a tree trunk for a man. Such is imagination according to Alain. As judgment, it involves in its very nature an assertion of existence, which cannot be blocked by Alain's distinction between inwardly and outwardly oriented imagination. An object posited as real is thus the beginning of the imaginary object. Imagination appears as a succession of momentary little dreams followed by rude awakenings. This *assertive* character of imaginative thought is perhaps even more marked in Alain than in psychologists who admit a reviving sensory content at the base of images. For these latter psychologists, judgment (if considered an autonomous spontaneity) can stand over against the image. We can exercise the Stoic *epoche,* we can abstain. The image would not thereupon vanish, since it is first and foremost a sensory content. It would remain as an inexistent [*un irréel*], and thus would don once again its essential character, which is precisely nonexistence. For Alain, on the contrary, the constitutive factor of the act of imagining is judgment. Consequently, there are only two alternatives. Either one is *in* the imaginative act, and we *perceive falsely.* Or else we wake up, we are *outside* the imaginative act, we correct our judgment, there are no more fictions, there is only reality and true judgment. Regarding dreams and waking life, good enough. But daydreaming, be it noted, is not dreaming. A man who goes off into a daydream tells himself stories *which he does not believe,* yet which are something other than mere abstract judgments. Here is a kind of assertion, a type of existence midway between the false assertions of dreams and the certitudes of waking life, a type of existence which is evidently that of imaginary creations. To make judgmental acts of these is to attribute too much to them.[38]

But also it is to attribute too little to them. One must consult the data of consciousness. There is a fact, called an "image," and this fact is an irreducible structure of consciousness. When I evoke the image of my friend Peter, I do not make a false judgment about a state of my body. Rather, my friend Peter *appears to me;* not, to be sure, as *some thing,* as actually present, as *there.* But he appears to me *in image* [*en image*]. Doubtless I must shift to reflection to formulate the judgment, "I have an image of Peter," directing my attention not to the object of the image but to the image itself as a psychic reality. But this shift to reflection in no way alters the positional [39] quality of the image. I do not wake up, I do not right myself, I do not suddenly *discover* that I formed an image. Quite the contrary, the moment I make the assertion, "I have an image of Peter," I realize that *I knew all along it was an image.* Only I knew it in a different fashion, for this knowledge was one with the act by which I constituted Peter in image.

An image is an undoubted psychic reality. An image can in no way be reduced to a sensory content, or be constituted on the ground of a sensory content. These are the points which, we hope, must be acknowledged at the close of this critical exposition. If we wish to go further, we shall have to go back to experience and describe the image in all its concreteness, as it appears to reflection. But how avoid making the mistakes we have noted? Neither the experimental method of the Würzburg school nor pure and simple introspection will do, for we have seen that they cannot avoid metaphysical prejudgments. Are we not face to face with a radically impossible task?

Perhaps, however, error does not creep into the reflective act itself. Perhaps error appears at the inductive level, when, on the basis of facts, one establishes laws. If so, would it be possible to create a psychology which would remain a psychology of experience,[40] yet would not be an inductive science? Is there a kind of privileged experience which would put us directly in contact with the law? A great contemporary philosopher thought so, and we shall now ask him to guide our first steps in this difficult science.

CHAPTER IX

The Phenomenology of Husserl

The great event of pre-World-War-I philosophy was certainly the appearance of the first volume of the *Jahrbuch für Philosophie und phänomenologische Forschung* containing the principal work of Husserl, "Ideen zu einer Reinen Phänomenologie und Phänomenologischen Philosophie." [1] This book was destined to revolutionize psychology no less than philosophy. Doubtless phenomenology, the science of pure transcendental consciousness, is a radically different discipline than the psychological sciences, which study consciousness and the being of man indissolubly linked to a body and confronting a world. Psychology, for Husserl, remained like physics or astronomy "a science of the natural attitude," [2] that is to say, a science involving a spontaneous realism. Phenomenology, on the contrary, begins when we "take out of play the general positing of existence which belongs to the essence of the natural attitude." [3]

The essential structures of transcendental consciousness, however, do not disappear when this consciousness immures itself in the world. The chief findings of phenomenology remain valid for the psychologist, *mutatis mutandis*. The very method of phenomenology may serve as a model for psychologists. The essential phase of this method is doubtless "reduction," *"epoche,"* that is to say, the bracketing of the natural attitude,[4] and of course the psychologist does not perform this *epoche,* but remains on the terrain of the natural attitude. Nevertheless, there are methods available to the phenomenologist after reduction that could be of use to the psychologist. Phenomenology is a description of the structure of transcendental consciousness based on intuition [5] of the essences of these structures. This description takes place, of course, on the level of reflection; but reflection must not be confused with introspection, which is a special mode of reflection aimed at grasping and establishing empirical facts. To transform the results of introspection into scientific laws there must ensue an inductive transition to generality. There is another type of reflection, utilized by the phenomenologist, which aims at the discovery of essences. That is to say, it begins by taking its stand from the outset on the terrain of the universal. Though proceeding in terms of examples, little importance is attached to whether the individual fact which serves as underpinning for the essence is real or imaginary. Should the "exemplifying" datum be pure fiction, the very fact that it was imaginable means that it embodied the sought-for essence, for the essence is the very condition of its possibility.

> Hence anyone fond of paradoxes may say in strictest truth, provided he understands the ambiguity attaching to the term, that "fiction" is the vital element of phenomenology as of all eidetic science,[6] the source from which knowledge of "eternal truths" draws its nourishment.[7]

What holds for the phenomenologist holds also for the psychologist. To be sure, we do not want to deny the essential role of experimentation and induction in all their forms in establishing a psychology. But before experimenting, must one not know as exactly as possible *what* one is going to experiment *upon?* On this matter experiment can provide only obscure and contradictory information.

> The great era (of the physical sciences) began in modern times when geometry, which had already been developed on pure eidetic lines to a high pitch of perfection in the ancient world (and in its essentials in the school of Plato), was suddenly widely invoked for purposes of method in physics. It was realized that the essence of the physical thing is to be *res extensa* [an extended object], and that geometry is consequently an ontological discipline relating to an essential character of things: spatial structure. But it was further realized that the generic essence of a thing comprises many other structures, as is amply demonstrated by the fact that scientific development immediately struck out in a new direction. The aim was to establish a series of new disciplines to be coordinated to geometry, with the vocation, likewise, of rendering rational the data of the empirical level.[8]

Husserl's words on physics may be applied to psychology as well, which will make great strides when it ceases to burden itself with ambiguous and contradictory experiments, and starts bringing to light the essential structures constituting the subject of its investigations. We have seen, for example, that the classical theory of the image harbored implicitly a whole metaphysics, and that experimentation was undertaken without discarding this metaphysics. A host of prejudices, originating sometimes as far back as Aristotle, were thus imported into the experiments. But could we not ask first, *before* resorting to experiments (whether these consist in introspective experimentation or any other procedure), *what an image is?* Does this element of psychic life which is so important have an essential structure accessible to intuition and specifiable in words and concepts? Are there assertions incompatible with the essential structure of an image? In a word, psychology is an empirical discipline that is still looking for its eidetic [9] principles. Though often unfairly charged with being hostile in principle to this discipline, Husserl proposed rather to be of assistance. He never denied that there is experimental psychology, but he believed that to remedy the most serious deficiency one must establish an eidetic psychology. Naturally, such a psychology would not borrow its methods from the mathematical sciences, which are deductive, but from the phenomenological sciences, which are descriptive. It would be a "phenomenological psychology," investigating and specifying essences on the intramundane level,[10] as phenomenology does on the transcendental level. And indeed we must continue to speak here of experience, since every intuitive seeing of an essence remains experiential. But it is an experience that altogether precedes experimentation.[11]

A study of the image must therefore be an attempt to carry out a phenomenological psychology on a particular point. One must try to set out the eidetic of the image, that is to say, fix upon and describe the essence of this psychological structure as it appears to reflective intuition.

Then, only after having established the set of conditions which a psychic state must fulfill in order to be an image, one should pass from the certain to the probable in order to learn what experience can teach us concerning images as presented in a contemporary human consciousness.[12]

Husserl was not content, however, to provide only a method, with regard to the problem of images. The *Ideas* contains bases for an entirely new theory of images. Actually, Husserl touched on the question only in passing; and, as will be seen, we do not agree with him on every point. Moreover, his remarks need deepening and completing. But the observations he made are of the highest importance.

The fragmentary nature of Husserl's observations renders an exposition of them particularly difficult. A systematic framework should not be sought in the following paragraphs, but only a set of fertile suggestions.

The notion of *intentionality* gives a new conception of images. For Husserl, as we know, every state of consciousness—or rather, following German usage, every *consciousness* [13]—is consciousness *of* something.

> **All *Erlebnisse* which share this essential trait are also called "intentional *Erlebnisse*." To the extent that they are consciousness of something we may say that they are "intentionally referred" to that something.[14]**

Intentionality, such is the essential structure of all consciousness. A radical distinction naturally follows between consciousness and that of which there is consciousness. Whatever it may be, the object of consciousness is as a matter of principle outside consciousness (except in the case of reflective consciousness), or is transcendent. This distinction, to which Husserl never wearied of returning, aimed at combating the errors of a certain immanentism which would constitute the world with *contents* of consciousness (for example, Berkeleyan idealism). No doubt there are contents of consciousness, but these are not the object of consciousness; for through them intentionality sights the object, which in turn is the correlate of consciousness, but is not *of* consciousness. Beginning with the ambiguous statement that "the world is our representation," psychologism banishes the tree I perceive in a myriad of sensations, colored impressions, tactile and thermal impressions, etc., which are "representations." Eventually, the tree appears as a sum of subjective contents, and becomes itself a subjective phenomenon. Husserl, on the contrary, begins by putting the tree outside us.

> **It is an absolutely universal rule that a *thing* cannot be given in any possible perception, that is to say, in any possible consciousness whatsoever, as really immanent.**[15]

To be sure, Husserl does not deny the existence of visual or tactile data which constitute a part of consciousness as immanent subjective elements. But these are not the object. Consciousness is not directed toward them; rather, through them it aims at the external thing. This visual impression which is currently part of my consciousness is not *the red*. The red is a quality of an object, a transcendent quality. This subjective impression which is no doubt an "analogue" of the red of the thing, is only a "quasi-red." That is to say, it is the subjective matter, the *"hyle"*,[16] on which operates an intention transcending itself and trying to snare the red out there.

> **One must always keep in mind that the impressional data whose function it is to "profile" the color, the surface, the shape [17] (that is to say, which have the function of "representing") are radically distinct in principle from the color, the surface, the shape, in short, all the qualities of the thing.[18]**

The consequences for images are immediately apparent. An image, too, is an image *of* something. We are dealing, therefore, with a certain consciousness of a certain object. In a word, the image ceases to be a psychic *content*. It is not *in* consciousness in the guise of a constitutive element. Rather, in the consciousness of a thing in image [*d'une chose en image*] Husserl distinguished, as in perception, an imaging intention and a *hyle* enlivened [19] by the intention. The *hyle* naturally remains subjective, but by the same token the object of the image, unattached to the pure "content," resides outside consciousness as something radically different.

> **(Might it not be objected that . . .) a flute-playing centaur, a fiction which we freely feign, is, by that very token, a free composition of representations within ourself? We shall reply: Certainly, . . . the free fiction is spontaneously undertaken, and what we engender spontaneously is, to be sure, a product of the mind. But as for the centaur playing the flute, it is a representation if we mean by "representation" what is represented and not if we mean by "representation" a psychic state. The centaur itself is, of course, not something psychic. It exists neither in the soul nor in consciousness nor anywhere. It does not exist at all, it is invention through and through. More precisely: the state of consciousness of invention is invention *of* the centaur. To**

> **that extent, no doubt, we may say that the "meant-centaur," the "invented-centaur," belongs to the *Erlebnis* itself. *But let us not confuse the* Erlebnis *of invention with that which has been invented as such.*[20]**

This is a key passage. The nonexistence of the centaur or of the chimera does not entitle us to reduce them to mere psychic functions. No doubt on the occasion of these non-existents there are real psychic formations. The error of psychologism is apparent, for the temptation was strong to leave these mythical beings to their unreality and to regard only psychic contents. But Husserl restored to the centaur, in the very heart of its "unreality," its transcendence. Irreality [*néant*], if you please: but by that very token it is not in consciousness. Husserl did not discourse further on the structure of the image, but his contribution to psychologists is readily gauged. By becoming an intentional structure the image has passed from the condition of an inert content of consciousness to that of a unitary and synthetic consciousness in relation with a transcendent object. The image of my friend Peter is not a dim phosphorescence, a furrow left in consciousness by a perception of Peter. It is an organized form of consciousness which refers in its own way to my friend Peter; it is one of the possible ways of aiming at Peter. Thus, in the act of imagination consciousness refers to Peter directly, not by means of a simulacrum *in* consciousness. At one stroke vanish, along with the immanentist metaphysics of images, all the difficulties adduced in the preceding chapter concerning the relationship of the simulacrum to its real object, and of pure thought to the simulacrum. That "Peter in reduced format," that homunculus carted about by consciousness, was never *of* consciousness. It was an object in the physical world that had strayed among psychic realities. By expelling it from consciousness and asserting that there is but one Peter, the object of perceptions and images, Husserl freed the psychic world of a weighty burden and eliminated almost all the difficulties that clouded the classical problem of the relations of images to thoughts.

Husserl did not stop there with his suggestions, however. In effect, if an image is but a name for a certain way in which consciousness takes aim on its object, nothing prevents us from aligning physical images (paintings, drawings, photographs) with images termed "psychic." Psychologism, curiously enough, had ended up radically separating them from each other, even though it finally reduced psychic images to physical images *in ourselves*. Also, on this latter doctrine one could not even interpret a painting or a photograph except by consulting the mental image which it evoked by association. For all practical purposes this was an infinite regress, since the mental image was itself deemed a photograph; another image would be needed to interpret this one, and so on. By contrast, if an image is a certain way of animating intentionally[21] a hyletic content, the apprehension of a portrait *as an image* could well be assimilated to the intentional apprehension of a "psychic" content. It would simply be a matter of two different species of "imaging" consciousness. The germ of this assimilation may be found in a passage in the *Ideas* which should become a classic. Husserl analyzed the intentional apprehension of a Dürer engraving:

> **Let us consider the engraving by Dürer, "The Knight, Death, and the Devil." We may distinguish first of all the normal perception, the correlative of**

> **which is the *thing* which is the "engraving," this sheet. In the second place, we find the perceptual consciousness in which, through these black lines and little colorless figures, "Knight on horseback," "Death," and "Devil" appear to us. In aesthetic contemplation we are not directed to them as objects, but as realities which are represented "in image"; more precisely, we are directed to the "imaged" realities (*abgebildet*), the knight in flesh and blood, etc.[22]**

This passage can form the basis for an *intrinsic* distinction between images and perceptions.[23] Granted, the *hyle* we grasp in constituting the esthetic manifestation of the knight, death, and the devil is unquestionably the same as in a pure and simple perception of the page. The difference lies in the intentional structure. The important thing to Husserl in this connection is that the "thesis" or positing of existence undergoes a neutralizing modification.[24] This need not concern us at the moment. It is enough to note that the [intentionally animated] matter is not sufficient by itself to distinguish images from perceptions. Everything turns on the way in which this matter is animated, that is to say, on a form which is born in the intimacy of the structures of consciousness.

Such were the brief allusions made by Husserl to a theory which was doubtless developed in greater precision in his courses and unpublished papers, but which is quite fragmentary in the *Ideas*. Its helpfulness to psychology is incalculable, but all the issues are far from being clarified. We see now that an image and a perception are two different intentional *Erlebnisse* distinguished above all by their intentions. But what is the nature of imaginative intending, and how does it differ from perceptual intending? A description of essences is evidently needed. Lacking any further account by Husserl, the task must fall to us.

Moreover, an essential problem remains unsolved. Following Husserl, we were able to outline a general description of an important intentional class comprising images known as "mental" and (for lack of a better term) images which may be called "external." We know that an "external-image consciousness" and the corresponding perceptual consciousness, though different in intention, have an identical impressional matter or "stuff." Black lines serve as well for constituting the image "Knight" as for the perception "Black marks on a white page." But is this also true of mental images? Do these have the same *hyle* as do external images, that is to say, ultimately, as do perceptions? Some passages in the *Logische Untersuchungen* [25] seem to encourage us to think so. Husserl declared that images have the function of "filling out" empty conceptions [*savoirs vides*], as do the *things* of perception. For example, if I think of a swallow, I may think it vacuously, that is to say, merely engender a signifying intention focused upon the word "swallow." But to fill out this empty awareness, turning it into an intuitive awareness, it is of no consequence whether I form an image of a swallow or whether I see a swallow in flesh and blood. This filling-out of the meaning by the image seems to imply that the image has a concrete impressional matter or "stuff" which, like perception, is itself a fullness.[26] Furthermore, in his *Vorlesungen zur Phänomenologie des inneren Zeitbewusstseins* ["Lectures on the Phenomenology of Inner Time-Consciousness"] Husserl distinguished between retention, which is a nonpositing[27] way of preserving for consciousness the past as past, and recollection, which consists of making reappear past *things* with their qualities. The latter is "presentification" (*Vergegenwärtigung*),[28] and involves the repetition, though in a modified awareness, of all the original perceptual acts. For example, if I have seen a lighted theater, I may reproduce in memory either the lighted theater ("There was a show at the theater that night . . .") or the perception of the lighted theater ("Strolling by that night *I saw* the lighted windows . . ."). The latter is *reflecting in memory,* because the reproduction of the lighted theater implies for Husserl reproduction of the perception of the lighted theater. The memory-image is thus nothing but a perceptual consciousness modified by the coefficient of pastness. It would seem, therefore, that while laying the groundwork for a radical reformulation of the question Husserl remained a prisoner of the old conception, at least with regard to the *hyle* of the image, which was for Husserl a reviving sensory impression.[29] But if so we are about to encounter difficulties analogous to those which plagued us in the preceding chapter.

First of all, on the phenomenological level, after the reduction has been effected, it would seem to us rather difficult to distinguish by intentionality between images and perceptions whose matter is identical. For having put the world "between parentheses," the phenomenologist does not lose it. The distinction "consciousness / world" loses its meaning, and the line is now drawn differently. The set of *real* elements of the conscious synthesis (the *hyle* and the various intentional acts which animate them) are distinguished from the "meaning" or "sense" [*Meinung, Sinn*] which inhabits the consciousness. The concrete psychic reality is to be called *noesis,* and the indwelling meaning, *noema.* For example, "perceived-blossoming-tree" is the noema of the perception I now have of it.[30] This "noematic meaning" which belongs to every real consciousness, however, is itself *nothing real.*

> Every *Erlebnis* is such that in principle there is always the possibility of directing one's gaze either to it and its real components or in an opposite direction, to the noema, for example, the perceived tree as such. In the latter case our glance encounters, in truth, an object in the logical sense, but one which could not exist of its own accord. Its *esse* consists solely in its *percipi.* But this formula must not be taken in the Berkeleyan sense, because the *percipi* does not contain the *esse,* in this case, as a real element.[31]

The noema is thus an irreality [*un néant*], with only ideal existence similar in type to that of the Stoic *lekton.*[32] The noema is simply the necessary correlate of the noesis.

> The eidos of the noema relates to the eidos of the noetic consciousness. They imply each other eidetically.[33]

But in that case how distinguish after reduction between the centaur I imagine and the blossoming tree I perceive? The "imagined centaur" is also the noema of a fulfilled noetic consciousness.[34] It, too, is nothing, exists nowhere, as we saw a while ago. But before reduction we were able to find in that very unreality a way to distinguish a fiction from a perception, for the blossoming tree existed somewhere outside us. We could touch it, clutch it, turn away from it, then, retracing our steps, come upon it again in the same spot. The centaur, on the contrary, was nowhere, neither in me nor outside me. Bracketed now, the tree-*thing* is now known only as the noema of our actual perception, and thus is an irreality [*un irréel*], just like the centaur.

> The tree pure and simple, the tree in nature is as far as possible from this "tree-perceived-as-such" which belongs as "that-which-is-perceived" to the meaning of the perception in an inalienable manner. The tree plain and simple can burn, can break down into its chemical components, etc. But the meaning—the meaning of *this* perception, an element which belongs with necessity to its essence—cannot burn, has no chemical components, has no power, no real properties.[35]

Where, then, is the difference between them? How can there be images and perceptions? How can we rediscover a real world and an imaginary one after the barrier of phenomenological reduction has been lifted?

Everything hinges on intentionality, it will be replied, on the noetic act. Have you not said yourself that Husserl did the groundwork for an intrinsic distinction between images and perceptions, a distinction in terms of intention rather than matter? Husserl himself distinguished in *Ideas* between the noemata of images, of memories, and of perceived things.

> It may be in each case a matter of a blossoming tree and that tree may appear in each case in such a manner that a faithful description of *that which appears* as such would have to use scrupulously the very same terms. Yet the noematic correlates are not for all that any less different, on essential grounds, when we are treating of perception, imagination, imaginative presentifications, memory, etc. Now the apparition is characterised as "reality in flesh and

> **blood," now as fiction, now as presentification in memory, etc.[36]**

But how interpret this? Can I animate any impressional matter whatsoever as perception or image, at will? What would "image" or "perceptual object" mean in that case? Need one only refuse to relate the noema "blossoming-tree" to preceding noemata in order to constitute an image? No doubt this is the procedure before the Dürer engraving, which we can perceive at will as a thing-object or as an image-object. Naturally, this is a question of two interpretations of one and the same impressional matter. When it is a question of a mental image, however, we can all ascertain that it is impossible to animate the *hyle* so as to make it matter for perception. Such hyletic ambivalence is possible only in a small number of privileged cases (paintings, photographs, copies, etc.) Even if the alternatives were available, one would still have to explain why my consciousness intends some matter as image rather than as perception. The problem is one of what Husserl called "motivations." And certainly we can see that the animation of the impressional matter of the engraving rendering it an image depends on extrinsic motives (because that man couldn't be there, etc.). Thus we meet once more the extrinsic criteria of Leibniz and Spaier. But if the same is true of mental images, we are brought by a side road back to the difficulties of the preceding chapter. Then, the insoluble problem was that of finding the characteristics of a true image. Now, the problem becomes that of finding motives for forming "matter" into a mental image rather than into a perception. In the first case the answer was that if the psychic contents are equivalent there is no way to discern the true image. In the second case the answer must be that if the matter is of the same nature there can be no valid motive.

To tell the truth, there is in Husserl the hint of a solution. The fiction, "centaur playing a flute," is aligned in *Ideas* with the operation of addition. In both cases, consciousness is "necessarily spontaneous," whereas for the consciousness of sensory intuition—empirical consciousness—spontaneity is out of the question. Later, in *Cartesian Meditations,* Husserl distinguished between passive syntheses taking place by association, whose form is temporal flow, and active syntheses (judgment, fiction, etc.).[37] All fictions would be active syntheses, products of our free spontaneity, and all perceptions, on the contrary, would be purely passive syntheses. The difference between fictional images and perceptions would therefore spring from the fundamental structure of intentional syntheses.

We subscribe completely to this explanation, but find it quite incomplete. First, does the fact that images are active syntheses involve a modification of the *hyle* or only a modification of the type of unification? One might easily conceive an active synthesis compounding reviving sensory impressions. Spinoza and Descartes explained the fictitious in this fashion. A centaur would be constituted by the spontaneous synthesis of a reviving perception of a horse and a reviving perception of a man. But one might also suppose [38] that the impressional matter of perceptions is incompatible with the intentional character of a fiction-image. Husserl does not go into this issue. In any case, the result of his classification is to separate sharply memory-images from fiction-images. We saw above that the memory of a lighted theater was a "presentification" of the thing ("lighted theater") together with a reproduction of the perceptual operations. This is definitely passive synthesis. But there are so many intermediate forms between memory-images and fiction-images that this sharp separation is unacceptable. Either both are passive syntheses (which is, in sum, the classical position) or both are active syntheses. In the first case, we return by a side road to the classical theory; in the second case, we must give up the theory of "presentification," at least in the form Husserl gave it in *Vorlesungen zur Phänomenologie des inneren Zeitbewusstseins.* In any event, we are brought back to our primary observation: the distinction between mental images and perceptions cannot derive from intentionality alone. A difference in intention is necessary but not sufficient. The matter must also be different. Perhaps the matter of images must even be itself a spontaneity, but of a lesser type.

In any case, Husserl blazed the trail, and no study of images can afford to ignore the wealth of insights he provided. We know now that we must start afresh, setting aside all the prephenomenological literature, and attempting above all to attain an intuitive vision [39] of the intentional structure of the image. It also becomes necessary to raise the novel and subtle question of the relations between mental images and "physical" images (paintings, photographs, etc.) [40] We should also compare image-consciousness and sign-consciousness, in order to free psychology once and for all from the egregious error of making images into signs and signs into images. Finally and above all the *hyle* peculiar to images should be examined. It might be that on the way we would have to leave the realm of eidetic psychology and resort to experimentation and inductive procedures.[41] But eidetic description is the required starting point. The way is open for a phenomenological psychology.

CHAPTER X

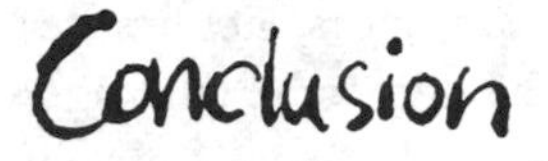

Every psychic fact is a synthesis. Every psychic fact is a form, and has a structure. This is common ground for all contemporary psychologists, and is completely in accord with the data of reflection. Unfortunately, these contentions have their origin in a priori ideas. In agreement with the data of inner sense, they do not originate there, in inner experience. Psychologists have thus resembled in their undertakings those mathematicians who wanted to retrieve the continuum by means of discontinuous elements. Psychic synthesis was to be retrieved by starting from elements furnished by a priori analysis of certain logical-metaphysical concepts. The image was one of those elements,[1] and reveals, in our opinion, the most decisive rout experienced by synthetic psychology. The attempt was made to soften the image, to refine it, to render it as fluid and as transparent as possible, so that it would not *prevent* syntheses from taking place. And when certain writers realized that even thus disguised, images were bound to shatter the continuity of the psychic stream, they rejected images entirely, as pure Scholastic entities. But they failed to realize that their criticisms had to do with a certain conception of images, not images themselves. All the trouble lay in having come to images with the idea of synthesis, instead of deriving a certain conception of synthesis from reflection upon images. The problem raised was the following one: How can the existence of images be reconciled with the requirements of synthesis? They failed to realize that an atomistic conception of images was already contained in the very manner of formulating the problem. There is no avoiding the straightforward answer that so long as images are inert psychic contents, there is no conceivable way to reconcile them with the requirements of synthesis. An image can only enter into consciousness if it is itself a synthesis, not an element. There are not, and never could be, images *in* consciousness. Rather, an image is *a certain type of consciousness.* An image is an act, not some thing. An image is a consciousness *of* some thing.

Our critical investigations cannot go further. A phenomenological description of the structure known as "an image" would have to be the next step. This will be attempted in another work.

Notes

Notes to Chapter I

1 The traditional formulation of what Sartre means by the notion of being independent of spontaneity was usually couched in terms of will. What I perceive when I look at, say, a sheet of paper, is perfectly independent of my will or anyone else's will. Traditional notions of will, however, suggest some specific function of the mind, and also imply reflective and deliberate mental action. Sartre prefers the term "spontaneity," to suggest the underived character of mental activity or consciousness in all its forms and at all levels. The spontaneous is that which is activity through and through, thus utterly lacking in passivity, and entirely transparent to itself because it contains no foreign elements. Such is for Sartre the nature of consciousness.—Tr.

2 The term "inert" connotes events dependent on external relations rather than on internal relations, as in the physical law of inertia, according to which the motion of an object remains unaltered until some *outside* force causes a change.—Tr.

3 The fundamental distinction of Sartre's *L'Être et le néant* is employed here. (Paris: Gallimard, 1943; *Being and Nothingness,* tr. Hazel Barnes, New York: Philosophical Library, 1956.) There are realities which exist *in themselves;* i.e., in their being they are

"wholly at one with themselves." Such is everything except consciousness, whose being is always and necessarily "for itself," a spectator of itself, so to speak, and thus "outside" itself rather than "in itself." Sartre's rejection of the notion of unconscious mind is based on the impossibility of anything being at once "in itself" and "for itself," at once a thing and a mental act.—Tr.

4 As the example shows, the prototype of the image in this work is what later is characterized (in Chapter IX) as a "mental image," rather than an image built upon perception.—Tr.

5 This principle is absolutely fundamental to the entire argument and critique in the present work, although all its consequences are not developed until Sartre's later works (especially, *L'Imaginaire,* Paris: Gallimard, 1940 [*Psychology of the Imagination,* New York, Philosophical Library, 1948], and *L'Être et le néant*).—Tr.

6 The thing and its image may well have the very same character, the same "whatness," and therefore, when one abandons an image-consciousness in order to theorize about images, one is liable to assume incorrectly that sameness of character means sameness in type of existence. Whether or not a thing and its image have the same sort of being is far from being decided by their identity of character or "whatness." The correct decision in this case, Sartre is maintaining, can only be made phenomenologically, that is, by reflective observation of a "thing-consciousness" (perception), an "image-consciousness" (imagination), and their respective objects.—Tr.

7 We are notified by the parenthetical clause that Sartre's analysis has undercut the conventional distinction between atomism and rationalism, and has placed them in the same bin, so to speak, so far as theory of imagination is concerned.—Tr.

8 *"La psychologie positive"* connotes in French thought those schools and aspirations of psychology that are "antimetaphysical" or "antiphilosophical," that are "empirical" in the special sense of emulating the methods of the physical sciences, that are generally "physicalist" and "reductionist."—Tr.

Notes to Chapter II

1 *du monde intérieur.* The sentence as a whole suggests that this is a misprint for *"du monde extérieur,"* "from the external world."—Tr.

2 Otherwise stated, even an iconic sign is such only for an interpreter who has some reason, not motivated by the character of the icon itself, for correlating it to something signified. A map of Colorado can function as an iconic sign of the terrain of the state of Colorado only if I am informed by the name "Colorado" and by the printed scale, conventions of coloring, etc., what it signifies and how to correlate the map to the terrain. These indispensable pieces of additional information are clearly not elements or relations within the map as an icon. Thus, there are no *natural* icons, or icons capable of functioning as such apart from some arbitrary convention or learned custom.—Tr.

3 Contrary to what Sartre says here, it would seem that Hume regarded the differentiation between impressions and ideas as immediately given, at least in "normal" cases. But in any case Sartre would argue that Hume's account of the difference in terms of "vivacity" and "faintness" cannot measure up to the facts of experience and does not reveal the basis of the spontaneous discrimination.—Tr.

4 The reference is presumably to Hume.—Tr.

5 Cp. Descartes, *Meditation II.*—Tr.

6 *les faits psychiques.* We have followed Sartre throughout in the use of the term "psychic" rather than "psychological," because "psychological" may mean all sorts of things in current speech, from neural reflexes as in physiological psychology to racial symbols as in Jungian depth psychology. "Psychic," on the other hand, suggests more specifically the realm of the mental, the realm of consciousness or awareness.—Tr.

7 For an illustrious case of this belief, see for example, Clark Hull, *Principles of Behavior* (New York: Appleton-Century, 1943), p. 13: "The rules of logic are more dependable, and consequently less subject to question, presumably because they have survived a much longer and more exacting period of trial than is the case with most scientific postulates."—Tr.

8 "There is nothing in the intellect which was not first in the senses."—Tr.

9 See above, ch. I, n. 8.—Tr.

10 A being who views himself as in a world is ***not in*** it, or *of* it, in the same sense that an object is, and no science which is truly *empirical* would blind itself to this peculiarity of human beings except out of an unreasoning passion to make all sciences "objectivistic," sciences of "objects-of-and-in-the-world-*simpliciter*." For Sartre, and for most phenomenologists and existentialists, the point is a central one for any true science of man.—Tr.

11 As G. E. Moore pointed out, yellow is indefinable (unanalyzable).—Tr.

12 An actual intuition is any awareness which is fulfilled by being confronted "in person" by the object or state of affairs in question; for example, grasping the mathematical state of affairs that 2 plus 2 make 4 (rather than merely writing the formula correctly), or seeing my friend Peter (rather than merely referring to him in a conversation). No single term is more central to phenomenology and more alien to current trends in British and American philosophy than the term "intuition." Its exposition would merit an essay. The interested reader is referred to the classic discussions by Edmund Husserl in *Ideas* (New York: Macmillan, 1931), § 1–4, 7 & 18–24. Perhaps the essential point to be stressed here is that for the phenomenologist the primary mode of evidence is intuitive. An intuition (summarily explained) is an act of consciousness by which the object under investigation is *confronted,* rather than merely indicated *in absentia.* Thus, it is one thing merely to indicate the Pantheon (merely "to have it in mind," as we say) and another to confront the indicated object by an act of imagination or perception. The indicative act is "empty"; the intuitive act is "filled out." Once this distinction has been made, it would seem difficult for even those persons most wary of the term "intuitive evidence" to deny that every cognitive inquiry must ultimately rest its claims on acts of intuition, even if supplementary modes of evidence (e.g., inductive inference regarding

the external world which is confronted by perceptual intuition) must be invoked to develop the inquiry. For an object must be present, confronted, to be investigated, however far from such original confrontation or intuitive grasp the investigation may have to roam as it proceeds. In the physical sciences, the reliance in the last analysis upon perceptual intuitive evidence is patent. In psychology and phenomenology, as in every science claiming to be rational, intuitive evidence is likewise fundamental; and also, of course, constitutes one of the topics of these sciences. Owing to the impracticality of a detailed account in this place, it may be helpful to note briefly some familiar senses of "intuition" which would be quite out of keeping with the phenomenological usage. First, intuitive knowledge has no traffic with mystical insight. The "filling out" of a previously "empty" consciousness of an object represents a logically distinct kind of consciousness, not some flow of feeling. Second, intuition is not an identification with the object in the Bergsonian sense. Third, intuition is not limited to the familiar type of intuition of the external world which we call "sense-perception," but may be directed to consciousness itself, to complex states of affairs, and to universals. Fourth, almost invariably to intuit an object or state of affairs is not to know its existence (the exception concerns reflective intuition of the "specious present"). Fifth, to intuit an object is not necessarily to know everything about it, viz., the inadequacy of sense-perception with respect to the full nature of its object.—Tr.

13 "or in the intellect itself." See above, n. 8.—Tr.

14 In the French sense of "classical," which generally refers to the seventeenth and eighteenth centuries of European thought.—Tr.

Notes to Chapter III

1 Binet, *Psychologie du Raisonnement,* Paris, 1896.

2 Much interest was shown in an attempt by Ahrens, a Belgian, to develop a new theory of images in his *Cours de Psychologie* given in Paris in 1836 and published by Brockhaus and Avenarius.

3 In this phrase Sartre reveals his pluralistic conception of scientific method, in opposition to any claim to reduce all the sciences to a single science and to a single empirical method treating a single type of object.—Tr.

4 "Critical" is presumably used here in the sense of Kant's Critical philosophy.—Tr.

5 *De l'Intelligence,* 1871, Vol. I, Preface, pp. 1–2.

6 Though experience was conceived here in far too limited a fashion.

7 Taine, *op. cit.,* p. 9.

8 The importance of this point in relation to the existentialism of Sartre's major philosophical work, *L'Être et le néant,* has not been sufficiently noted. See also below, ch. IX, n. 26.—Tr.

9 See p. 21.—Tr.

10 Galton, "Statistics of Mental Imagery," *Mind,* 1880; "Inquiries into Human Faculty and Its Development," *ibid.,* 1885.

11 Binet, *Psychologie du raisonnement* (Paris, 1896).

12 Cp. Lachelier, *Psychologie et métaphysique.*

13 Batbie Report, November 26, 1872.

14 Much misunderstanding of Sartre's philosophy is based upon a confusion between ordinary introspective inquiry and the special reflective method of phenomenology. The difference turns on the method of phenomenological "reduction" by which one suspends one's spontaneous realism, or what George Santayana called one's natural "animal faith" in the existence of things. For a detailed discussion of the difference between introspective and phenomenological investigation, see Husserl, *Ideas, op. cit.* For a brief account of phenomenological reduction, see below, ch. IX.—Tr.

15 Cp. Aristotle, *De Anima,* III, 8, 432a, 8: "When the mind is actively aware of anything it is necessarily aware of it along with an image."

16 Brochard, *De l'Erreur,* p. 151 (our italics).

17 Named after work first carried on at the University of Würzburg in Germany, by students of Ostwald Külpe (1862–1915), during the first decade of this century.—Tr.

18 Ribot, *La Vie inconsciente et les mouvements* ["Movement and the Life of the Unconscious"], pp. 113 et seq. In this portion, Ribot attempted to refute the conclusions of the Würzburg psychologists that there exist imageless thoughts.

19 Ribot was in effect to contest the significance of the Würzburg experiments.

20 See above, ch. I, n. 8, and ch. II, n. 10.—Tr.

21 Cp. *L'Imagination créatrice,* pp. 17 et seq.

22 *Ibid.,* p. 20.

23 *Logique des Sentiments,* p. 22.

Notes to Chapter IV

1 The *durée,* "duration," or "enduring" of consciousness as understood by Bergson is a flowing process, as opposed to a succession of separate events. Cp. Bergson, *Introduction to Metaphysics* (New York: Liberal Arts Press), *passim.*

2 Annales Médico-Psychologiques, 1925.

3 Journal de Psychologie, April 15, 1926. See also an attempt at a Bergsonian interpretation of hallucinations in Lhermitte, *Le Sommeil.*

4 *Matière et mémoire,* p. 22.

5 *Ibid.,* p. 24.

6 See below, ch. IX. The use of the term "a consciousness" is awkward in English, of course, as it is in the French as well (*"une conscience"*). The justification for such an awkward term was later given by Sartre in *L'Imaginaire, op. cit.,* page 11, as follows: "We have taken the liberty of using the term 'consciousness' with a somewhat different meaning than usual. The term 'state of consciousness' implies, with respect to psychic structures, a sort of inertia, a passivity which seems to us inconsistent with the data of reflection. We shall use the term 'consciousness,' not to designate the monad and the ensemble of its psychic structures, but to name each of those structures in its concrete particularity. Thus we shall speak of 'image consciousness,' 'perceptual consciousness,' etc., drawing upon one of the German meanings of the word *Bewusstsein.*" From this usage, it seems appropriate to

pass to the term "a consciousness," thus avoiding the static term "a state of consciousness."—Tr.

7 Perhaps the effect of the interior of a highly decorated Byzantine church such as San Vitale in Ravenna would serve as an analogy.—Tr.

8 The emphasis in the question is on *prendre,* connoting an active function.—Tr.

9 Regarding the awkward term "a consciousness," see above, n. 6.—Tr.

10 "Le Souvenir du présent" ["The Present as Remembered"] in *L'Énergie spirituelle* [Paris, 1920; also, in *Revue philosophique,* December 1908].

11 *Matière et Mémoire, op. cit.,* p. 80.

12 "Le Souvenir du présent," *loc. cit.*

13 See below [in ch. IX, on Husserl] the meaning of this distinction, which is forced on anyone who attempts to envisage the relationship of consciousness to the world. [Roughly speaking, the noema is the object-pole of consciousness, and noesis is the subject-side, as distinguishable in reflection after the phenomenological "reduction" mentioned in ch. III, n. 14, above.—Tr.]

14 *Matière et mémoire, op. cit.,* p. 180.

15 "L'Effort intellectuel," in Bergson, *L'Énergie spirituelle, op. cit.* (our italics).

16 Here and elsewhere the term "schema" is used to refer to a sort of guiding model for mental activity, neither particular nor universal, as in the Kantian notion of a schematism of the imagination. The term used by Sartre is *schème.*—Tr.

Notes to Chapter V

1 Prior to World War I.—Tr.

2 Spaier, "L'Image mentale," *Revue philosophique,* 1914.

3 See ch. IV, n. 16.—Tr.

4 Sartre uses the French term *médium,* and places it between inverted commas, perhaps with the intention of punning on the two meanings of an intermediary and an occult medium. See the subsequent reference to a "daemon."—Tr.

Notes to Chapter VI

1 See above, ch. III, n. 17.—Tr.

2 A free translation and commentary of *Logische Untersuchungen* (rev. ed., Halle, 1913–21) was made by Marvin Farber under the title of *The Foundation of Phenomenology* (Cambridge, Mass.: Harvard University Press, 1943).—Tr.

3 Bühler, "Tatsachen und Problem, etc.: Intergedanken," *Arch. für ges. Psychologie,* IX, 1907, 321.

4 *Étude expérimentale de l'intelligence,* 1903. The choice of subjects as too young, and the choice of tests as much too easy, have often been criticized. Cp. Ribot, *La Vie inconsciente et les mouvements.*

5 See ch. I, n. 8, above.—Tr.

6 Cp. C. I. Lewis, *Analysis of Knowledge and Valuation* (La Salle, Ill.: Open Court, 1946): "No limited number of tests would completely exhaust [the] significant content of any empirical objective belief" (p. 246); "Fully to corroborate [the statement, 'Tomorrow will probably be fair'], would require observation of all such tomorrows throughout all past and future time [p. 317]."—Tr.

7 *L'Âme et le corps,* Paris, 1908. Binet died in 1911.

Notes to Chapter VII

1 Spaier, "L'Image mentale," *Revue philosophique,* 1914.

2 Philippe, *L'Image.*

3 William James, *Psychology—Briefer Course* (New York: Holt, 1892), p. 165 (cited by Meyerson in Dumas, *Nouveau traité de psychologie,* vol. II).

4 Alfred Hoernlé, "Image, Idea and Meaning," *Mind,* January 1907, p. 75 (cited by Meyerson in *loc. cit.*).

5 Spaier, *La Pensée concrète,* p. 201.

6 Meyerson, *loc. cit.,* p. 578.

7 *Ibid.,* p. 582.

8 *Ibid.,* p. 588.

9 See above, ch. IV, n. 1.—Tr.

Notes to Chapter VIII

1 Cp. for example Maldidier, "Les Caractéristiques probables de l'image vraie" ["The Probable Char-

acteristics of True Images"], *Revue de Métaphysique,* 1908.

2 Spaier, *La Pensée concrète,* p. 121.

3 The example discussed by Spaier, *loc. cit.,* is precisely of this sort. [Sartre's presentation of Taine's "second solution" has some terminological difficulties that we have done our best to interpret correctly.—Tr.]

4 Spaier, *Ibid.,* p. 121.

5 Taine, *De l'Intelligence,* vol. I, p. 125.

6 *Ibid.,* p. 89.

7 *Ibid.,* p. 99.

8 *Ibid.*

9 *Ibid.,* p. 101.

10 *Ibid.* "This is the specific counteragent [*le réducteur spécial*], that is to say, the contradicting sensation."

11 *Ibid.,* p. 115.

12 *Ibid.,* p. 117.

13 *Ibid.,* p. 120.

14 See above, ch. II, n. 12.—Tr.

15 We cannot be certain that Spaier would have endorsed without qualification the theory just expounded, but we intended chiefly to characterize a tendency and to describe a viewpoint widespread today.

16 Spaier, *op. cit.,* p. 121. (Italics in the original text.)

17 See in this connection the interesting observations of Lagache on the role of respiratory rhythm in auditory hallucinations, in *Les Hallucinations verbales et la parole* ["Verbal Hallucinations and Speech"], Paris, 1934.

18 See above, ch. II, n. 12.—Tr.

19 Meyerson, in Dumas, *Nouveau traité de psychologie,* vol. II, p. 594.

20 See Sartre, *Psychology of the Imagination, op. cit.,* Part 2, Sec. V.—Tr.

21 The remark appears suggestive in connection with esthetic perception; or, as Sartre would be more inclined to say, "esthetic imagination" (see *Psychology of the Imagination,* "Conclusion," Sec. II).—Tr.

22 This sense of "matter," as the "stuff" of an experience,

should not, of course, be identified with matter in the physical meaning. In ch. IX, such "matter" and a Greek word, *hyle,* will be used synonymously.—Tr.

23 "Intention" refers here and subsequently to the "pointing," "aiming," or "prepositional" feature which animates or enlivens the "matter" or "stuff" of consciousness (in John Dewey's language, mind is "mind*ing*"), and which varies in its type with different experiences.—Tr.

24 See above, ch. IV, n. 8.—Tr.

25 See above, ch. IV, n. 16.—Tr.

26 Claparède, *L'Association des idées* ["The Association of Ideas"], 1903.

27 As announced several pages earlier.—Tr.

28 Cp. the description of this passive genesis in Husserl, *Cartesian Meditations.* [This excellent English translation, published by Martinus Nijhoff, The Hague, is by Dorion Cairns. I have to thank Prof. Stanley Pullberg for acquainting me with it just before the completion of the present translation.—Tr.]

29 To be distinguished, following Husserl, from absolute or phenomenological consciousness.

30 See above, this chapter.—Tr.

31 Moutier, *L'Aphasie de Broca* ["Broca Aphasia"], ch. VII, "Des Images Verbales" ["Verbal Images"].

32 The behaviorists' denial of the existence of images is also based on methodological considerations, and ultimately on metaphysical grounds. "I would like to reject images entirely," wrote Watson, "and show that all thought is naturally traceable back to sensori-motor processes seated in the larynx." Cp. *Behavior,* Vol. I; and "Image and Affection in Behavior," in *Journal of Philosophy,* July 31, 1913.

33 *Système des beaux-arts* ["System of Fine Arts"], p. 22.

34 *Quatre-vingt-un chapitres sur l'esprit et les passions* ["Eighty-One Chapters on the Mind and the Passions"], p. 41.

35 *Système des beaux-arts,* p. 16.

36 The trade name of a popular French beverage.—Tr.

37 *Les Propos d'Alain* ["Discourses by Alain"], *Nouvelle*

revue française, Vol. I, p. 33. Analogous ideas are to be found in *La Pensée qui guérit* ["Thought That Heals"] by Dr. Pierre Vachet.

38 It may be objected that there are judgments of possibility and probability. But these offer no resolution of the problem. To say "What I see there may be a man" and to imagine the figure of a man while daydreaming, are evidently two very different operations. Alain's thesis, moreover, implies an unacceptable view of the perceptual act, as we have shown already.

39 The "positional quality" of an act of awareness refers to the positing of one or another type of reality-status with respect to the object of awareness (as certainly existing and "there," as possibly existing, as nonexistent, etc.) In the present case, the point is that the object of prereflective imaginative consciousness is posited as "merely imagined," and a subsequent reflective judgment that I am imagining does *not* wrench me from some previous state of deceptive credulity—rather, I was conscious *all along,* not only of *what* I was imagining, but also *that* I was imagining it.—Tr.

40 The French word *expérience* may mean experiment, experience, or both at once, depending on the context.—Tr.

Notes to Chapter IX

1 Published in English translation as *Ideas* (New York: Macmillan, 1931; tr. W. Boyce Gibson). Subsequent references are to the § numbers which are common to editions in all languages.—Tr.

2 Cp. *Ideas, op. cit.,* § 30.

3 Cp. *ibid.,* § 32.

4 This procedure is, so to speak, a "step back" from belief concerning what exists in nature, including belief affirmative, negative, conjectural, dubious, judgmental, or prejudgmental, whether it be directed toward material objects, toward minds (including one's own), or toward selves (including one's own person), regardless of the plausibility or implausibility of any such belief. In "stepping backward" one does not contest any factual belief. One would be justified, after all, in contesting a factual belief, such as the belief that there are

rivers in nature and that they flow downhill, only on the basis of contrary evidence. Moreover, even if some evidence were presented that rivers do flow uphill after all, I do not suppose that I could bring myself to disbelieve on the spot what I have believed so firmly for so long, in order to believe otherwise. The procedure of "reduction," *epoche,* or "bracketing," then, does not require disbelief, or even prolonged doubt, regarding the presumed facts of nature. Rather, one "steps back," as it were, from the "natural viewpoint" of factual belief. The "natural" viewpoint is "natural" in two related senses: it is usual, owing no doubt to the practical demands of living; and, unlike the "reduced" viewpoint, it is concerned to discover what exists in nature. After the *epoche,* however, all such "natural" beliefs merely lie before me, so to speak, like the chains of a prisoner who has slipped out of them: quite intact, but no longer binding.

Perhaps the most efficient introduction to the *epoche* or "phenomenological reduction" is that presented by Husserl in *Ideas* (*op. cit.*), § 31.—Tr.

5 See above, ch. II, n. 12.—Tr.

6 "Eidetic" in the sense of sciences concerned with essences or *eide*. Mathematical sciences are eidetic sciences. But unlike mathematics, phenomenology is not a merely *formal* eidetic science. Its theme consists of the essential structures of something which is not merely ideal, namely, consciousness as intentional experience.—Tr.

7 Cp. *Ideas, op. cit.,* § 70.

8 Cp. *ibid.,* § 9.

9 On "eidetic," see above, n. 6.—Tr.

10 This sentence appears to describe approximately the nature of Sartre's later work, *Being and Nothingness,* which is a kind of "phenomenological anthropology" developed from the standpoint of phenomenological reduction or *epoche,* and descriptive of "man-in-the-world," with special focus on what might be called "personal consciousness" (which includes as a feature the sense of other persons in the world).—Tr.

11 See above, ch. VIII, n. 40.—Tr.

12 The program which was actually carried out in *Psychology of the Imagination, op. cit.*—Tr.

13 See above, ch. IV, n. 6.—Tr.

14 Cp. *Ideas, op. cit.,* § 36. The term *Erlebnis,* untranslatable into French [or English . . . —Tr.] comes from the verb *erleben. Etwas erleben* means "to live something." *Erlebnis* has approximately the meaning of *vécu* [lived through] as used in Bergsonian philosophy.

15 Cp. *ibid.,* § 42.

16 For the usage of the terms *hyle* and "matter" here and subsequently, see above, ch. VIII, n. 22.—Tr.

17 The German terms *Farbenabschattung, Glätteabschattung,* etc. are untranslatable. [The notion common to all these terms (see the German verb *sich abschatten*) is that the "reddish" and "squareish" and "smoothish" data yield up the object itself and its particular properties of redness, squareness, and smoothness "in profile"; otherwise stated, such data are so many "facets upon" (*not* "facets of") the particular object and its particular properties.—Tr.]

18 Cp. *Ideas, op. cit.,* § 41.

19 *Beseelen* [to besoul]. Cp. *Ideas, passim.*

20 Cp. *Ideas, op. cit.,* § 23 (our italics).

21 On "intention," see above, ch. VIII, n. 23.—Tr.

22 Cp. *Ideas, op. cit.,* § 111.

23 A distinction, however, that Husserl did not develop further in his works published to date [1936].

24 The aim was chiefly to show that in esthetic contemplation the object is not posited as existing. His descriptions are oriented rather to the Critique of Aesthetic Judgment. [On "positing," see ch. VIII, n. 39.—Tr.]

25 In the revised, postwar edition which takes cognizance of progress made by Husserl since the first [pre-World-War-I] edition.

26 This contention, which we shall try to refute later, has in any event the great merit of making the image something other than a *sign,* in contrast to contem-

porary British and French psychology. [The refutation is to be found in *Psychology of the Imagination,* and introduces the notion of a negating or "nihilating" capacity of consciousness, which leads directly to the problem formulated in the title of Sartre's major work, *Being and Nothingness.*—Tr.]

27 On "positing," see ch. VIII, n. 39. Retention, unlike memory, is a manner of "keeping in mind" the immediately "past" *without* positing it, *without* having it as a terminus of awareness or object. Thus, retention "nonpositionally" carries the immediate past (ever changing, of course) along with it, much as a ship necessarily draws in its wake water just traversed; whereas memory posits the past much as the lookout on the mast may face the stern and fix his gaze on an object left behind in the distance.—Tr.

28 Or, "bringing-to-presentness."—Tr.

29 We readily acknowledge that we are presenting an interpretation justified but not demanded by the passages in question. It remains true that the text is ambiguous and that the question is one which calls for a firm and clear account. [Sartre's *Psychology of the Imagination* is his attempt to provide such an unequivocal account for phenomenology.—Tr.]

30 We are expounding crudely a very subtle theory whose detailed character does not directly concern us here.

31 Cp. *Ideas, op. cit.,* § 98.

32 Cp. Diogenes Laertius, 7. 43 & 63.—Tr.

33 Cp. *Ideas, op. cit.,* § 98.

34 I may heed an object such as the flowering tree in my garden merely in the sense that my awareness indicates it for me "emptily," as when I remark to a visitor, "I have a flowering tree in my garden"; I may then go into the garden and heed the same object in a perceptual act, in which case my formerly "empty" awareness is "fulfilled" or is an "intuition" as the object confronts me "in person." But, Sartre is asking, since Husserl considered an imaginative act a "fulfilled" type of awareness, how could one ever distinguish after "reduction" or *epoche* between reduced

perceptual consciousness and reduced imagining consciousness? Both, it would appear, would now be equally "realistic" in appearance.—Tr.

35 Cp. *Ideas, op. cit.*, § 89. [Reading *essence* for Sartre's typographical error *sens,* in accordance with the original German text of Husserl.—Tr.]

36 Cp. *ibid.*, § 91.

37 See above, ch. VIII, n. 28.—Tr.

38 As we tried to demonstrate in the preceding chapters.

39 See above, ch. II, n. 12, and this chapter, n. 34.—Tr.

40 *l'image matérielle.* Presumably this term is synonymous with the term "external images" distinguished earlier in this chapter from "mental images." Taken literally, the term is of course contrary to the entire position adopted by Sartre in this work.—Tr.

41 Undertaken later by Sartre in *Psychology of the Imagination, op. cit.*—Tr.

Notes to Chapter X

1 See for example the conclusion drawn by Burloud in *La Pensée d'après Watt, Messer et Buhler* ["Theories of Thinking in Watt, Messer and Buhler"], p. 144: "Two things [must] be distinguished in thought: its *structure* and its *content.* The content consists of sensory elements or relational elements or both at once. The structure is nothing but the way in which we are aware of this content."